Big Plants for Small Budgets

How to Grow Outdoor Plants Indoors

Big Plants for Small Budgets

How to Grow Outdoor Plants Indoors

By Chuck Crandall

with Barbara Crandall

 Chronicle Books / San Francisco

Acknowledgements

Special thanks are due Larry Steedley and Don Ross of ITC
Garden Center, Los Angeles, and their helpful staff; to Don
Shinkle, Sr., Don Shinkle, Jr., and Jo Shinkle of Valley Garden
Supply, North Hollywood, and their great staff; and to George
Gable of Mordigan Nurseries, Los Angeles, who provided help
and endured numerous photographic invasions.

Printed in the United States of America.

ISBN O-87701-052-8

Published by Chronicle Books
870 Market Street
San Francisco, California 94102

Contents

Previous Books by the Author
Success with Houseplants
They Chose to Be Different

Introduction

This book is written for, and dedicated to, the growing legion of plant-loving students and other young people struggling along through a hard, cruel world in pinched poverty (we were there, once); newlyweds who are still scraping by on a meager salary; retired people who found the promise of years of ease after lifelong toil a cruel hoax played on them by rampant, spiraling inflation; and any others who love to have green, growing things around them, but find the cost of beautiful houseplants a luxury too dear for their limited budgets.

Within these pages, you will find hope—and help. You'll learn not only how you can have large foliage plants which rival those in the most elegant homes or swank office suites and lobbies, but also how to grow unusual, exotic species that are seldom, if ever, found indoors. And every plant or tree described herein can be bought for *under* ten dollars, some for under five!

Primarily, this book covers the large foliage specimens—plants and trees that dominate an entire corner, an entry, or a window. Many are traditional outdoor plants that with a little patience and care can be acclimated to life indoors. Some are sub-tropical plants and others are tropicals, brought here from other parts of the world and termed "exotic," as opposed to "native." These are often grown both indoors and out in mild-climate areas. You'll learn how to adapt the less expensive outdoor "field-grown" specimens to flourish in your living room. This often means you can have, for a pittance, the same plant that sells in plant boutiques and florist shops for fifty to eighty dollars.

So, read on, then get growing!

Chuck Crandall
Barbara Crandall

"Plants were the primary furnishings in our first home," say the Crandalls, "because we couldn't afford Knoll furniture and had to fill the empty rooms with something beautiful." Their love for plants goes back to childhood, but it wasn't until they met and married, they say, that they discovered their mutual affection for plants and periodically went beserk in nurseries and plant shops. Whatever they could fit into the back seat of their Volkswagen (with the sunroof open), they bought. One day they counted their leafy "offspring" and found they had adopted nearly 200 plants and trees—a wall-to-wall forest that eventually crowded them out of a one-bedroom house. "Wouldn't it have been easier to sell or give away some of the plants to make more room for living?" a friend asked them at the time. "Bite your tongue!" was their unequivocal response. Nearly every plant or tree in their collection was purchased at a nursery as a traditional outdoor plant. With tender care, they were able to adapt these specimens to thrive indoors.

"Big Plants for Small Budgets" was written for other plant-lovers to guide them in acquiring and growing indoors a wide variety of inexpensive outdoor plants.

Chapter 1

Tiffany Shopping on a Woolworth Budget

Big, beautiful houseplants have become fashionable all over the world. Houseplant growers who would have settled for an African violet and a fern not long ago now want the largest, lushest plants they can find, or in some cases, can afford.

This trend has had the predictable effect of driving up the price of almost all plants, causing those of us who have been collecting plants for years to gnash our teeth in anguish. Plants we used to find tagged at three or four dollars are currently selling for eight, ten, or even fifteen dollars. Inflation had little to do with the jump; it was the age-old law of supply and demand.

Houseplant cultivation and marketing has become a billion-dollar industry in a very few years. Plant shops that, in addition to plants, carry everything from macramé pot hangers to wheelbarrows are being added to staid, conservative department stores; plant boutiques which offer pampered and exotic specimens are flourishing in unlikely places all over the globe; and even many nurseries that previously didn't want to bother with the houseplant shopper have capitulated and are now offering a good selection of species.

All of this is good for newcomers to plant collecting, for it opens up new sources and makes it easier to acquire unusual specimens. But spiraling prices have forced many seasoned collectors to propagate their own plants or seek new sources.

It was this set of circumstances that led us, a few years ago, into experimenting seriously with comparatively inexpensive field-grown outdoor plants to determine which varieties could be acclimated to indoor cultivation. We were delighted to find that with a little patience and care virtually any traditional outdoor plant or tree can adapt to interior environments. Since most of these plants are cheap in comparison to greenhouse-grown houseplants, with the right growing conditions one could live in a forest or garden of wall-to-wall plants and trees for a cost of about $200.

Inexpensive plants and trees. There are two categories of inexpensive, large foliage plants: 1) traditional outdoor species that can be, but seldom are, acclimated to indoor culture; and 2) field-grown sub-tropicals and tropicals that are intended for exterior landscaping use, which can also be easily adapted for living indoors. A secondary source is propagation from seeds, cuttings, and root-divisions, which requires months or sometimes years of care while waiting for impressive results, but which eliminates the need for an acclimation period.

Outdoor plants. There are literally hundreds of outdoor plants, shrubs, and trees which *could* be grown indoors with a lot of determination and horticultural skill, but we'll concentrate mostly on those species which adapt easily and are evergreen, retaining their foliage the year around. Deciduous species that drop their leaves seasonally are more trouble than they're worth, with a few exceptions.

Exotic and native tropicals and subtropicals. New Englanders and others who live in the northern portion of the United States will be familiar with these species only as hothouse plants, because the harsh northern winters preclude the exterior use of such tender species. But Californians, Floridians, and those who live along the Gulf Coast should find these plants and trees, intended for landscaping use, readily available at their nurseries. Some of these include *Cordyline stricta, Fatsia japonica*, and some uncommon palms rarely attempted as houseplants.

Almost without exception, these species and many others will be stocked in two places at the nursery. The field-grown plants which have been "hardened off" (acclimated to the harsh exterior environment of hot sun, cool nights, and wind) will be stocked under lath outside. The greenhouse-grown versions of the same plants, which would die in short order if exposed to sun and temperature extremes, will always be cloistered inside. These specimens were grown specifically for interior use and, unlike their hardier brothers, will adapt without difficulty to the dim light levels and dry air of the buyer's home.

If one can find the same type of plant either greenhouse-grown or field-grown, why not buy the greenhouse variety and eliminate the need for an acclimation period? Why not, indeed—if money is no object. There is, however, inevitably a vast difference in price between the two types. For example, we recently found a nursery that was selling beautiful *Dracaena marginatas* in five-gallon cans outside under lath. Each can had two plants, both three-and-a-half feet tall, and we estimated their age at about four years. (*D. marginatas* are slow growers.) These scarce, highly desirable beauties were going for the paltry sum of ten dollars per can. On the inside were smaller, less mature, greenhouse-grown specimens ticketed at forty dollars apiece. As it turned out, the canned specimens we bought required absolutely no acclimation period. They took to the inside just as eagerly as their greenhouse-pampered brothers would have.

Another example is the nine-foot-tall *Cordyline stricta* we found in a northern nursery. It had several volunteers (offsets) about three feet tall and had been at the nursery so long the can had rusted through. The price? Fourteen dollars. A comparable greenhouse specimen would have brought eighty to ninety dollars. It, too, adapted to living inside virtually overnight.

Problems and solutions. In addition to the "softening off," or acclimation process, outdoor plants and trees present a few additional problems, none of which is insurmountable. For example, there is usually some foliage damage from rough handling, wind, sun, and insects, or there may be many more "bugs" in the can and on the foliage than there are on greenhouse specimens.

Foliage damage is usually not sufficient cause for rejecting a plant that is otherwise sound and thriving. Unless the plant is a slow grower, injured branches or leaves can be trimmed off and will be replaced in a few weeks. As a matter of fact, this manicuring will probably be beneficial to the plant and will produce a fuller specimen, since pruning often stimulates vigorous new growth and branching from dormant buds in most species.

Insect predators can also be dealt with in short order, provided the plant isn't so severely infested that it's beyond rescue. (See the section in this book on pests.) If this is the case, the deteriorated condition should be evident, and you should not buy the plant. While it is true that you may be able to save it, you'll be risking spreading the contagion among your other plants. If you suspect a newly acquired plant may be infested, but you're not sure, before you bring it inside wash the foliage with a solution of Ivory bar soap and warm water. Cover the top soil with aluminum foil to keep the suds out of the pot. Once you've covered all the leaves—both sides—and the stem, rinse off the residue with either a garden hose on low pressure or a hand atomizer. A quarter-teaspoon of ant poison sprinkled on the top soil and watered in should eliminate any pests in the can or pot. Don't arbitrarily spray the plant with a "bug bomb" or other insecticide. This is an overkill approach, wastes your money, and more importantly, endangers beneficial insects and birds. Nine times out of ten, the soap-and-water treatment is successful against everything but scale insects. And you'll find safe, organic ways to cope with those in the plant pest section of this book.

Where to find budget-priced plants and trees. Almost without exception, you'll find lower prices and a wider selection at a large metropolitan nursery. Conversely, you'll find, as a general rule, higher prices and a more limited selection at the plant specialty shops, plant department stores, and plant boutiques, since they concentrate primarily on conventional, greenhouse-grown houseplants. Nurseries seldom give their plants, particularly the ones earmarked for exterior planting, the kind of individual care and attention that plant shops do. Nurseries are volume dealers and usually don't keep a plant more than a few days before it's sold. That's why their prices are so appealing. Their profit margins are low and calculated on a fast-turnover basis. They rarely pot up from the can, which would add to the cost of a specimen, while plant shops almost always do. They don't have the time or the inclination, in most cases, to mist and prune each specimen in stock; plant shop proprietors have lots of time for this personal care.

This individual treatment, coupled with the low-volume nature of boutique enterprises, is reflected in the prices plant specialty shops charge. You must weigh the benefits of getting a plant which has been pampered and potted against the price differential of a canned nursery specimen which requires additional attention.

We should point out that there are exceptions, on both sides. Some boutiques can and do compete on price with nurseries and there are some nurseries who tag their stock higher than many plant specialty shops. But, the fact remains that nurseries are traditionally volume dealers in field-grown outdoor plants and trees, and these are what this book is all about.

Part of the satisfaction of collecting plants—for us, at least—is plant shopping. We usually set aside a whole Saturday for going from one nursery or plant shop to the next, seeking out bargains or hard-to-find specimens. This helps us keep abreast of new varieties, hybrids, and price structures for the various plants and trees.

When to buy. In most sections of the country, spring seems to be the ideal time to shop for new additions and for replacements for specimens which didn't winter well. There are seasonal plants which are available in mid-winter, but generally speaking, the best selection of the large foliage specimens is offered at the beginning of mild weather.

In California and other temperate areas, a fairly wide selection of most varieties can be found the year around. Even so, the inventories increase in size and selection in the early months of spring. There are two major advantages to buying in spring: 1) Prices are usually much lower when there is an abundance of stock on hand at the plant outlet; and 2) plants and trees are entering their period of vigorous growth and can cope much easier with the rigors of re-potting and acclimation.

You should try to visit the nursery or plant shop on the day stock is delivered from the wholesaler, or early the next day. This assures you of the first and best selection, before the specimens have been picked over. Most plant retailers get new material on Thursday or Friday, in time for the usual heavy weekend trade. Ask your favorite plant source when they receive deliveries, then plan your visit to coincide.

What if you don't see what you want? If you've got your heart set on a specific species, but you haven't been able to find it in any of the outlets, ask your nurseryman to order it for you. Usually, a particular nursery orders from their wholesaler only those species for which they have a substantial or continuing demand—stock they know they'll be able to move. If the plant you want is available from their wholesaler, most nurserymen are glad to order it for you and it should arrive with the outlet's next consignment.

If you don't have access to a large nursery, you may be able to order the plant from one of the sources listed in the back of this book. This may run the cost up a few dollars, since you'll be expected to pay the freight.

How to buy. What do you look for in a plant? First of all, you want thick, luxuriant, uniformly colored foliage. This means the plant is thriving. Fading edges, mottled centers, and widely-spaced leaves which aren't characteristic of the species are clues that something is amiss. Second, you should look for thick stems or trunks, the thicker and stouter the better. The tallest plant of the bunch may be the most appealing to the novice, but height is only a plus factor if the plant has the other hallmarks of a healthy, properly cultivated specimen. Widely spaced leaves and a spindly, leggy stem usually mean the plant was "brought along" too rapidly with extra doses of fertilizer. If there are others of the same species with foliage that is set closer to a thicker trunk, select one of these. It will grow into the kind of plant you want eventually; the "stringbean" one never will. Attractive branching is a third feature to seek out, if it's applicable to a particular species. Branching helps create the effect of more than one plant in the pot and is more eye appealing. Sometimes a plant will throw offsets, or volunteers, which are juvenile plants. That's a fourth feature to look for. It's like getting two or three plants for the price of one.

How to pick a plant or tree

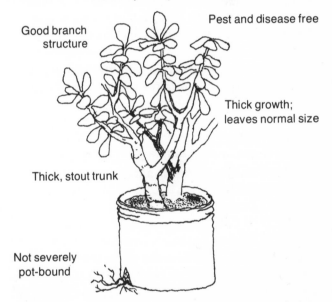

Good branch structure

Pest and disease free

Thick growth; leaves normal size

Thick, stout trunk

Not severely pot-bound

Finally, check the plant carefully for obvious signs of pests or other problems. Yellow or brown flecks on foliage that affect more than a few leaves is a tip-off that all is not well, and usually indicates the presence of thrips or spider mites. Curled or deformed leaves are a warning, also. Visible pests, such as aphids, scale or mealy bugs, which are all discernible with the naked eye, should send you elsewhere. A few chewed leaves are usually nothing to worry about. The predators who inflict this kind of damage are usually peripatetic vagrants who probably stopped for a quick snack and moved off to sample other delicacies nearby.

If not, you can see them plainly and deal with them easily. It's the fast-breeding, insidious, difficult-to-detect-until-it's-too-late invaders who colonize rapidly that you should avoid. Sunburned or wind-torn leaves are commonplace with field-grown specimens and can be pruned off. Provided most of the foliage is healthy and attractive, these minor flaws should not deter you from buying a plant.

You might also check to see how severely the plant is pot-bound (most canned nursery stock usually is, to some extent). A mild pot-bound condition is common and usually can be corrected by immediate potting on when you get the plant home. With a serious pot-bound condition, where roots are growing out in masses several inches long, it's a toss-up. You may be able to salvage the plant and then, again, it may be too far gone. Wholesale growers generally keep their plants pot-bound because this forces the plant to transfer its growth efforts to producing lusher, fuller foliage, instead of developing complex root systems. This makes the plant more attractive and easier to sell at the nursery.

A plant or tree can cope with this root-crowding for a time; in fact, certain species actually prefer tight shoes. But if the condition is not corrected soon enough, most specimens may not be able to recover. When a plant is acutely pot-bound, its feeder roots may be damaged or dried out and withered and no longer capable of gathering moisture and nutrients.

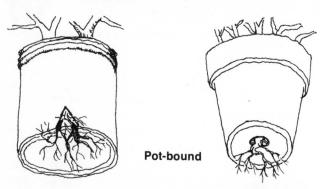

Pot-bound

So, as your final check, examine the drainage holes. A few roots jutting out are acceptable; a series of roots four or five inches long growing out of every hole, combined with lower leaves that are half the size of newer leaves, should be sufficient cause for you to pass up that specimen. That is not to say the plant is doomed. Plants struggle against tremendous odds to survive. If one root is dam-

aged, a plant will often develop two to replace it. Still, why risk your money and time on a plant of doubtful longevity?

What about "beat's me" plants? First of all, what's a "beat's me" plant? Well, this is any specimen you find in a nursery without a label which, when you ask the nurseryman what it is, he looks for the label, furrows his brow, shrugs and says, "Beat's me." This isn't a common occurrence, but it happens from time to time. The reason is that the grower (or wholesaler) delivered the plants to see how they would sell, but forgot to attach species labels. They are often hybrids or cultivars of established species but have foliage or structural characteristics which may differ radically from the true species. They are so new the nurseryman hasn't had a chance to bone up on them.

If you find "beat's me" plants under lath, you can assume they'll adjust indoors without difficulty, provided you give them basic care, as outlined in Chapter 5. If you like the plant and the price is right, go ahead and buy it. Then, ask the nurseryman to find out for you the botanical name and culture requirements. Armed with the name, you can research the plant yourself in "EXOTICA" or other horticultural references.

If, however, the plant is positioned in full sun, it may be wiser to wait to purchase until you learn the name and study up on the species to determine whether or not you can provide a good and proper home for it.

Occasionally, when nurserymen learn you intend growing a particular plant indoors, they'll tell you it can't be done and try to steer you to their houseplant inventory in the greenhouse. Some less diplomatic chaps may indicate their negative opinion about your potential success by casting aspersions on your sanity. Simply turn a deaf ear to all this well-intentioned counsel—in fact, it should reinforce your desire to succeed with the plant, particularly if the nursery staff start nudging each other, rolling their eyes or snickering under their breath.

What to do after you've bought. As soon as you get the plant home, either wash the foliage and stem as described earlier, or at least hose the foliage off. This will not only refresh the plant, it will also remove most transient bugs and/or pesticide residue which may be clinging to the leaves and stem.

Next, pour about a quart of lukewarm water on the top soil, wait fifteen minutes to half an hour, then pour in two quarts. The first quart dissolves any concentration of mineral salts (unused fertilizer) which has been used by the grower, and the next two quarts flush the salts out of the container.

Finally—and this may be the most difficult of all for you to do—pinch out or prune off the growing tips of the plant or tree. Do this *only* if you want to create a fuller specimen or to encourage branching. (See the illustration.) There are exceptions, and these should be obvious. The slow-growing species, such as dracaenas and *B. recurvata* would take months to show the beneficial results of

cutting back, and few of us are willing to wait that long. Also, never snip out the growing tips of a palm. If you do the trunk may die.

Special Note: Isolate any newly-acquired specimen for at least two weeks before introducing it to your other plants. A separate room is ideal; across the room or patio from other specimens is the next best location. Check the new plant daily —undersides of leaves, axils (point where branch and stem join) top soil, stem—for any signs of disease or pest infestation. Once the two-week incubation period has passed without incident, you can be reasonably certain the plant is horticulturally "clean."

Cutting back for fuller growth. Pinch out new leaves before they open.

These photos show the effects of pinching out new growth periodically. In the photo above, an avocado tree has developed two branches . . . in the photo on page 16, a *pseudopanax* has developed *five* new branches where one was pinched out.

Chapter 2

Acclimating Outdoor Plants to Indoor Environments

As a general rule, plants and trees that have been "hardened off" can't go from the nursery directly to the inside of your home. The key to your success in growing outdoor plants indoors is in adapting them to a new and hostile environment. While we may not think of our cozy living room as "hostile," a plant that has lived most of its life in the wind, rain, and sun is a dedicated outdoor type. It sometimes finds confinement indoors a devastating experience. Aged people who are suddenly uprooted from the familiarity and comfort of their lifelong home and moved to a strange, new environment often react the same way. The change is too sudden, too catastrophic.

As we've seen, some of the more adaptable species require little or no adjustment, but these are the exceptions. We have found it's almost axiomatic that plants and trees under lath or in full shade at the nursery are relatively easy to acclimate to life indoors, and plants in full or partial sun are generally the most difficult to adapt. The sun-lovers *can* adjust—it just takes a little longer to bring them around to your point of view. It required an entire year for us to successfully adapt a field-grown *Ficus benjamina*. It dropped nearly all its leaves for months, and new leaves never lasted more than a few days before they, too, fell. After making several trips outside to revitalize itself, it must have decided adaptation was better than continual motion sickness, and it grudgingly developed a sensible attitude.

The following procedures for adapting outdoor and field-grown plants, shrubs and trees are basic steps which have proved successful in the majority of cases. It should be noted that some specimens may never adjust to indoor environments, no matter how dedicated you are to the task. Pines, cypresses, and spruces, for example, simply will not accept interior environments for more than a month before the needles begin to fall.

While the acclimation procedures may seem complex and formidible, you'll find that, in the majority of cases, the plants and trees recommended in the last chapter for adapting to indoor use need little special care. With a few exceptions, most can go directly from the nursery to an indoor location. Detailed cultivation and acclimation requirements for each are included for precise guidance in selecting only those varieties for which you can provide the recommended care.

Acclimating sun-loving plants. Step One: Position the plant outdoors in the sun with about the same exposure it had at the nursery. Withhold water unless the plant is excessively dry, then water just enough to keep it from flagging, but keep the leaves misted. (Don't worry about the old saw that claims water drops on leaves act as magnifying glasses and cause sunburn. This is one-hundred percent emulsified bull.) Leave the plant in this location for about two weeks.

Step Two: If the plant is canned, select a container of the appropriate size (see the following chapter on potting) and pot it up. If you don't own a can-cutter, you can do the job with tin snips (which cost about two and a half dollars for a low-grade but adequate pair). If the plant is already potted up but not crocked (again, see the chapter on potting), you should re-pot properly.

Step Three: If the plant has continued to thrive after the re-potting operation for a week or ten days, move it to partial shade (dappled sun) for another ten to fourteen days. Increase the water volume slightly. Watch the plant carefully for paling foliage or excessive leaf drop. Loss of a few leaves is sometimes normal.

Step Four: Assuming the plant has continued to do well, move it to full shade and water normally. If you note signs of deterioration, move it back to partial sun until it recovers, then back to full shade. If it seems healthy and continues to produce new foliage after two weeks, you can take Step Five.

Step Five: Either move the plant indoors for its final and most critical adjustment period or leave it in shade outdoors until late fall before you attempt bringing it inside. When you do bring it in, position it within a foot or two of an east or north window, or at a west window with a thin curtain or shade to minimize the effects of the hot sun. The sun beaming through a west window in summer can build up temperatures as high as 120°. The plant should be able to handle—and probably prefers—full, unobstructed winter sun. Light is very important to sun-loving specimens. If you can't provide some sun, or very bright light, for at least five hours a day, you may not be successful with the sun-worshipers indoors.

Step Six: Now your work is cut out for you. There is just no way you can give the plant everything it needs so that it is fooled into thinking nothing has changed. It may not like the hot, dry air inside, so you'll have to keep the air around it as humid as possible. In addition to giving it a daily misting, put a pebble-filled tray under it and keep the pebbles moist. This will simulate, to some extent, the natural moisture content of the air outside.

Let's detour for a moment and discuss the creation of a microclimate using water-covered pebbles.

If you haven't had much experience with water in terra cotta saucers, you may not know that unglazed clay leeches moisture which can mildew a carpet or bleach a circle in a wooden floor. You can find at many nurseries and other plant outlets terra cotta saucers that have been glazed on the inside. This eliminates the moisture-damage problem very nicely, but these coated saucers are twice the price of unglazed clay.

The way to get around the premium price is to buy a can of masonry sealer, which is used to seal brick buildings so that moisture doesn't soak into the brick, and coat your own saucers. You can buy a quart can for about two dollars at most hardware and paint stores. It goes on easily with a paintbrush, and there's enough sealer in a quart can to cover the inside of approximately twenty ten-inch saucers.

Another type of pebble tray is a rust-proof wooden frame lined with galvanized tin. This requires someone in the household with basic carpentry skills and tools to build the framework, and also it is costlier. Tinsmiths are a vanishing breed. Most of this kind of work is now done by sheet-metal shops, which charge a steep price for custom work. But if someone in the family is handy, the metal can be purchased in sheet form, bent to fit the frame, and trimmed very easily with tin snips. The problem of sealing the corners can most expeditiously and inexpensively be solved by using one of the new epoxy glues that bond metal to metal.

Now, back to Step Six: The plant won't like the idea of a uniform temperature day and night, so you'll have to lower the nighttime temperature at least 10°, or preferably more. It probably won't be too fond of the low light level inside, either. You may think a room is bright, but compared to the light intensity outdoors, your home is viewed by most plants as not much more than a cave. If growth suddenly becomes willowy and leggy, the light level is insufficient. It never hurts and often

helps to supplement the available light indoors with a florescent lamp or a strong incandescent light, which you can leave on until late at night. Florescents work better because the tubes emit almost no heat and can be safely moved to within a few inches of the foliage. The ordinary filament-type bulbs produce enough heat to burn a leaf, so eight inches is about the minimum safe distance from the plant.

If you do use supplemental light, be consistent. Turn it on at the same time every day, and leave it on for the same length of time for maximum benefit.

Acclimating shade-loving plants. The shade fanciers are more educable to reason—they really will be much happier inside away from voracious insect attacks and inclement weather.

Step One: Pick a nice, shady spot on a porch or on a side of the house that is always in shade. Withhold water, but mist or hose-off the foliage daily, if the weather is hot, or every three days, if it is mild. You should detect no change in the plant other than a continuation of growth and good health. Leave the plant there for about a week.

Step Two: Re-pot, if necessary, as outlined in Step Two in the previous section.

Step Three: With a shade-loving plant, your choice of interior "trial locations" is much wider. Any window location (with the exception of an undraped west window in summer) should work. You may have some difficulty starting off with a location which gets less light, but perhaps not. Plants are individuals and don't always react the way all the experts tell them they must. Try the plant first where you'd like to keep it more or less permanently. It may adjust there without ado.

Troubleshooting. Some specimens may adapt without a whimper, dropping at most one or two leaves. Others may go into an absolute snit and not only drop dozens of leaves, but obstinately refuse to produce any new ones.

The most frequent discernible sign that the plant is not adjusting is drooping foliage. The branches may sag and the leaves may begin to curl under. This means the air is too hot and dry and is your cue to raise the humidity. If a plant totally collapses, you may have damaged the roots when you re-potted, sending the plant into shock. Only time will tell, and unfortunately this process is usually irreversible.

Even a plant that has been acclimated to indoor living will appreciate a vacation "back home" when mild weather comes. If you have a shady place on a deck, a patio, or a porch, move your adapted plants, which are now indoor-outdoor specimens, there for a month or two. This is especially beneficial for the ones which have fought hard against acclimation all winter and are mere shadows of their former selves. A trip outside will probably induce the recalcitrant plants to perk up and produce new foliage.

When you do put out specimens that have become accustomed to the interior of your home, only do so in mild weather when there is no danger of frost, and make sure they're not sitting in the sun, even for a few minutes. This, of course, is true also for conventional hothouse-grown houseplants, which are ultra-sensitive to the rays of the sun. Plants that have adjusted to the dim interior light are extremely sun-shy. Thinking that a short sunbath will revitalize a houseplant is misguided and potentially fatal.

Chapter 3

Re-potting Plants & Trees

Moving a plant from one container to another is a commonplace and frequently necessary indoor gardening chore. There is nothing difficult about it, but it must be done right, or there's the devil to pay, horticulturally speaking.

There are three primary reasons why you may have to re-pot a newly purchased plant: 1) Almost all plants bought from a nursery will still be in the can or a flexible plastic pot; 2) often, the plant will be "pot-bound," which means its roots are shooting out the drainage holes and need more room to roam for food and water; and 3) usually, if a specimen *is* potted up at the nursery, no crocking is added to prevent the drainage hole from getting clogged, which leads to root rot.

Potting from the nursery can.

Why re-pot a canned specimen? While it is true that a plant will survive for some months—even up to a year and longer—in the nursery can, there are several reasons why you should pot up in another container as soon as you can find the time: 1) Odds are better than two to one that the plant is pot-bound; 2) there is no crocking in the bottom of the can and the drainage holes may be stopped up, trapping stagnant water; and 3) there may be root-devouring insects in the can, since the plant was grown outdoors. You can't be sure the plant is not infested as long as it stays in the can. Also, 4) metal, obviously, is a non-porous material. Neither water nor excess nutrients can pass through metal. With a terra cotta or wooden container, water and nutrients leech easily through the porous material allowing the plant to "breathe"; finally, 5) a beat-up, dented metal can that has probably started to rust doesn't add much to an interior decor. Some people set the can inside a decorative container or paint it or adorn it with colorful contact paper, but—from a purely subjective point of view—we feel the can has served its purpose when we've brought the plant home and get rid of it as soon as possible.

Now, for a neat little contradiction, no one can say with exactitude that a plant won't thrive for years in a can. Some we've bought had been growing splendidly in their humble, rusted containers for at least three years. Re-potting from a five-gallon can is an expensive process, especially if you're a college student or newlywed living on a shoestring budget. Potting up into a terra cotta or ceramic container can cost more than the plant itself. As we get

deeper into the physiology of plants, you'll see why cans are unsuitable as long-term plant holders. Then you must decide for yourself whether to pot—or not.

Containers for plants.

Currently there are nine types of planting containers from which to choose: natural terra cotta (red or tan unglazed clay); glazed terra cotta (fired with a ceramic glaze that seals the microscopic holes which give pottery clay its porosity); rigid plastic; flexible (rubberized) plastic; wood; styrofoam; peat moss; metal; and wire basket containers lined with sphagnum moss.

Of all these containers, *natural terra cotta* is the best for most plants. Here's why. Part of the reason that plants growing naturally in the ground thrive is because they have good drainage and the ability to leech or throw off excess food, which is then dispersed into the surrounding soil. With terra cotta containers, which are porous, this natural process can be simulated. Excessively moist soil which can rot roots is almost never a problem in clay pots, provided the caretaker is practicing horticulturally sound watering procedures.

In a plant's natural habitat, rainfall is absorbed by the soil around a plant's root ball. Then as the soil dries out, air enters the pockets created by the shrinking soil particles around the roots, providing oxygen which is vital to the growth and well-being of healthy roots.

Because unglazed clay pots are porous, this leeching of excess food and water, and the ingestion of air, can be carried out efficiently by a plant. This is why the natural terra cotta pot has survived for ages as the most popular indoor-outdoor container for serious and knowledgeable gardeners.

Finally, with large plants and trees, the weight of clay pots stabilizes the plant and prevents tipping over, which damages the foliage.

So it should be obvious that we're prejudiced in favor of natural clay pots. This is not to say that containers of other materials are unsuitable. The point is simply that most plants seem to prefer life in a traditional terra cotta "home" than in a fancy, contemporary plastic "subdivision." Plants growing indoors have enough to cope with, so why not give them the kind of container they like best?

Let's examine the pros and cons of the other containers. First of all, let's look at *glazed terra cotta*. These are fine as decorative containers into which you set a plant already potted up in a natural clay pot. The fired-on glaze has sealed the clay and destroyed its porosity. Plants *have* been grown successfully for years in glazed containers, but their owners were careful how they fed and watered these specimens. Once they determined the right volume and frequency of water and plant food, they maintained this dietary program.

Glazed clay—like plastic, which we'll look at next—keeps the soil moist much longer, so root rot is a potential risk for those who give their plants a drink whether they're thirsty or not. The soil moisture problem is increased several times over when a plant is potted up in a glazed container without a drainage hole. This requires *dry welling*, putting a two-inch to three-inch layer of pebbles, broken crocks, or even rocks in the bottom of the pot before adding the potting medium and plant. Theoretically excess water drains down through the soil and into the dry well away from the plant's roots. Sounds great. Trouble is, you can't see how much water is trapped in the well and we all have a tendency to overwater. Water in a dry well evaporates very slowly. Each successive irrigation may raise the level of water until the entire root structure of the plant is submerged in a sloshy bog of stagnant water. This will invariably lead to soured soil and rotted roots, which in turn means an untimely death for another of our leafy friends.

If you already have a plant growing in a dry-welled pot, knock it out every three months or so and check the character and condition of the soil and the appearance of the roots. Is the soil swampy and does it give off a stench? Are the roots white and firm or brown and squishy? It is far better to underwater a dry-welled plant than to overwater. You can always add more if a plant seems to be suffering from dehydration, but—like trying to get toothpaste back into the tube—you can't remove excess water. Even better than this is to pot the plant up conventionally in a plain clay pot with a drainage hole.

Rigid plastic pots do serve a purpose in growing certain specimens which thrive in soil that is on the moist side. The so-called Spider plant (*Chlorophytum comosum*) as well as the Spathe and many ferns, to name a few, do quite well for years in plastic containers. This seems to be another contradiction after all the dialogue about the necessity of pot porosity and leeching of moisture and excess nutrients, but it really isn't. You

can achieve the same good results by growing these specimens in natural clay pots. You just have to water more often, sometimes every other day, and you can't hang the clay pots just anywhere as you can plastic, because of the weight problem. A freshly watered terra cotta container weighs *five* times as much as a just-watered plastic pot of the same size. So you must be careful about where and how you hang a clay container. The thunderous crash of a clay pot which has pulled out of its ceiling hook, taking the hook and plaster with it, and plummeted to the floor is not the best way to be awakened in the middle of the night out of a sound sleep, as we learned from experience years ago.

In addition to their inherent problems, rigid plastic pots lack stability and have an annoying tendency to topple—unless you've added several pounds of rock ballast before potting up in them, and this is only feasible with "grounded" plants. Also, plastic pots are thin and develop cracks easily if they're not handled gingerly.

Every year, more and more commercial growers of plants are switching from metal cans to **flexible plastic** containers. This change probably has a lot to do with the cost of metal compared to plastic. The flexible plastic pots are wholly unsuitable as permanent containers. First of all, they're not porous, and more important, because they're flexible, a plant's root ball gets crushed and compressed every time the plant is moved. Plants are not at all fond of root massage. Again, these containers are suitable only as temporary holding tubs until you can pot up into something else.

Wooden tubs and planters, of rot-resistant cedar or redwood, are popular with some indoor gardeners, but we've always felt they were more suitable for patios and porches. In the larger sizes, they are about the cheapest container one can buy or make. There is nothing organically wrong with wood; plants adapt quite well to it. Using them indoors is largely a matter of personal taste.

Styrofoam and **peat moss** pots, like metal and flexible plastic, should be viewed only as temporary containers. Styrofoam and peat moss share the flexibility problem of soft plastic, and peat moss collapses when soaked. You can pot up a plant that is in a peat moss container by potting container and all. The plant's roots grow through the moss after a few weeks and work their way into the new soil surrounding the moss. Eventually the peat moss decomposes in the soil, providing nutrient value for the plant.

We are seeing a revival of the traditional **wire basket** lined with **sphagnum moss** and filled with soil as a container for everything from ivies to wildflowers. The basket is covered inside with sphagnum moss which has been soaked in water, then a "pad" of soil is firmed in the bottom and one or more plants are added. Soil is then poured in and firmed and, as the soil level is built up, plants or flowers are added through the sides of the wire basket to create a hanging garden effect. The moist moss keeps the soil evenly damp, recreating the process that takes place when plants are growing naturally in the earth. The moss also does a good job of keeping the soil in the basket, so the basket can be hung inside. Ferns in particular do well in this setup.

Re-potting, step-by-step. (1) *Be prepared* with all the materials you'll need to do the job before you start. Select a pot about two inches larger than the old one (pots are measured from inside rim to inside rim) if the plant was potted up with crocking. If not, you may have to go up to a pot another inch or two larger to accommodate the additional bulk of the shards. If the plant is in a can or plastic tub, you may have to go up several sizes. Almost always the cans and tubs are cylindrical,

Select a container about two inches larger.

but the pots available are usually tapered. You can't force a plant to conform to the shape of the pot without inflicting serious damage on the delicate root system. In some areas of the country, cylindrical pots are available, which makes re-potting canned specimens a breeze.

If the plant is going to be hung, give some thought to wood or rigid plastic. As we've mentioned, a terra cotta pot puts a great deal of strain on a toggle bolt in a sheetrock ceiling. If you intend to suspend the plant from a rafter or beam, the weight of terra cotta is less of a problem. Some plastic pots come with saucers attached, which eliminates drip problems. About the only ways you can attach a terra cotta saucer under a clay pot is by wiring it to the pot, which isn't the most attractive rig in the world, or by suspending the plant in a macramé or rope hanger, which will hold the saucer firmly and becomingly in place under the pot.

Thoroughly water plant the night before.

You'll also need an adequate amount of a suitable soil mix (see the chapter on soils), clay shards to go over the drainage hole, a piece of lath or similar tool to firm the new soil around the old soil ball, and a container of diluted Vitamin B-1 solution or a similar booster to help the plant take the operation in stride.

(2) The day before you plan to re-pot, saturate the plant's old soil ball thoroughly with the Vitamin B-1 solution. Then saturate again a few minutes before you're ready to begin. This last irrigation will serve to loosen the soil around the edges of the pot or the can so the plant will release smoothly. A plant in a terra cotta pot that has not been watered prior to knocking out will probably not release, or because the dry soil is clinging tenaciously to the sides of the pot, it will come away leaving feeder roots imbedded in the dry soil that is still adhering to the interior walls of the pot. This is never a problem with plastic containers, since soil does not grip plastic.

Place crocking over drainage hole.

(3) Put the crocking material over the drainage hole or holes and add a pad of soil about three inches deep.

(4) *Metal cans:* Cut the can on opposing sides and pull the two halves away from the old soil ball. Obviously, you'll want to wear thick gloves for this operation. The cut edges of the can are sharp as razors. *Plastic tubs:* You don't have to cut plastic containers. Simply compress the sides gently inward all the way around, invert the tub with your hand over the top, as shown in the illustration, and the plant should slide out without difficulty. *Terra cotta pots:* Put your hand over the top of the pot, as shown, invert the pot and rap the top rim sharply against a firm surface. The plant should drop out, but you may have to rap it several times to free it. Once it's out of the pot, gently press the soil ball together to keep it from collapsing now that it is free of the confines of the container.

With larger (five gallon and up) tubs and pots, you'll have to lay the plant or tree on its side and ease the container away from the soil ball. Delicate foliage should first be tied up with strips cut from plastic refuse bags to prevent damage during this operation.

Now is the time to inspect the roots and soil ball for any signs of insect predators or other problems. In particular, check the bottom soil of plants that were sitting on the ground at the nursery. Grubs

Add sphagnum moss to keep soil from escaping through drainage hole.

Pour in a two-inch-deep layer of soil and firm.

Place hand over top soil, invert pot and rap rim sharply against table top or other rigid surface.

and slugs often get into a can through the drainage holes. Examine the roots by gently separating them to see if any pests are hiding there. Pick off anything that moves and destroy same by dropping it into a bucket of soapy water. If you see more than one or two invaders, you should consider taking stronger measures. (See the chapter on plant pests.)

While you're looking through the roots for pests, take a close look at the roots themselves. They should be white and turgid, if they're healthy. If they're brown or black and mushy at the tips, you have a case of incipient root rot. Hold back water, in this event, after you've potted on, and give the plant a longer period of drought (perhaps two weeks) to allow the root system to recover.

More extensive browning requires pruning off the decayed areas and sprinkling the affected roots with "Rootone," which is an antiseptic that is highly effective in treating ailing roots.

(5) Pick up the plant by the soil ball (never by the stem) and set it in the new container. The top soil should be three-quarters of an inch to an inch from the top rim of the pot. If it's as much as two inches or more below the rim, remove the plant and add more soil. If it's less, or if the plant is sticking up above the rim with its top soil exposed, you have to move up to a larger container. One way you can avoid this nasty little surprise is by measuring the

inside depth of the pot with its crocking and soil bed in place, then measuring the depth of the plant out of its original container to see if it will fit.

If you don't have a larger container on hand, don't wait until it's convenient for you to get one, unless you want to risk losing the plant. Once it's out of its container, the plant's root ball and soil dry out rapidly. Wrap the soil ball completely in a wet burlap bag or cloth and rush down to your source of horticultural supplies. Inevitably, this will happen late on Sunday or on a holiday when everything is closed, or just as a torrential rainstorm lets loose. In these situations, muttering profanities and/or kicking lots of stuff on the way to the nursery helps relieve some of the anger and frustration.

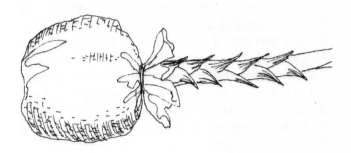

Assuming you have a container of the appropriate size and you've set the plant in its new home, pick up the container, with your thumbs resting on the top soil, and slam the base of the pot against a firm surface. This will "set" the plant in its pot. Make sure the plant is centered, then proceed.

(6) Pour in a layer of soil all around the edges and tamp it down firmly, rotating the pot as you go to keep the plant centered. Add another layer, pack it down, and continue the operation until you've reached the level of the old top soil. It is important to tamp the soil solidly as you go. Roots grow into new soil only if it is pressing tightly against them. A loose pack means that the roots will continue to turn inward, never benefiting from the additional growing room you've provided. This means the plant will never really achieve the kind of luxuriant growth you want or of which it is capable.

Plant drops out easily. Note pot-bound condition.

At this time you may "top dress" the plant. This means replacing the old top soil with fresh, nutrient-rich soil. If you decide to do this, remove the old top soil carefully so you won't damage any roots which may be growing just under the surface. Chopsticks are effective tools for safely breaking up crusty clods and a spoon works well for removing them. When you add new top soil, be sure to maintain the original soil level. If you raise the soil level, the plant may rot off at the stem. A good way to insure against this is to wrap a twist-tie firmly around the stem at the original soil line before you start.

Center plant in new pot and tamp down new soil all around.

(7) Now water the plant thoroughly until water pours out of the drainage hole. Then repeat. This accomplishes two things: first, it "weds" the old soil to the new, and second, it signals you that your drainage system is working efficiently. If no water drains out of the pot, poke a stick or screwdriver up through the drainage hole and jiggle the crocking material around. This should open up the dike. If it doesn't, you may have to knock the plant out again and rearrange the crocking shards.

If the plant is draining properly, set it aside for a few minutes, then check the top soil. In all probability the new soil will have sunk in spots below the old soil level. This is because the new soil hasn't been packed down by months of watering and settling. Simply fill the depressions to top-soil level and wet the plant down again.

Give the newly potted plant a long period of drought before irrigating it again. In fact, let it almost dry out. The drying action will stimulate the

Thoroughly water newly-potted plant.

the interior walls of an old pot is a trap for delicate feeder roots. They grow into this soil, and when you knock out the plant to pot on next year, these roots will be torn away, endangering the well-being of the entire plant. It is much easier to clean old pots when plants have just been removed from them and the clay is still moist, so scrub up as the last step of your potting on. Plastic pots are relatively easy to clean. A damp cloth is often all that's needed.

Mist to freshen foliage and remove dirt from leaves.

roots to penetrate the new soil, which is the whole point of potting on.

Three final admonitions . . . (1) **Start with a clean pot.** Old terra cotta pots are fine for potting on, but only if the patina of white stains (leeched-out salts) and green scum (algae that grow on leeched salts) is completely removed. Mineral salts which are heavily encrusted on the rim of a pot can burn foliage that comes in contact with them. Try soaking really cruddy pots overnight in scalding hot water and TSP or a strong detergent. This should soften up the crust to the point where you can remove it with a stiff-bristled or wire brush and a little scouring powder. Once all the scum is removed, rinse the pot several times in clean water to wash away all traces of chemicals and detergents and either let the pot completely air dry in the sun or dry it in a warm (350°) oven.

A dirty clay pot can't "breathe" or leech out excess salts and moisture. Soil that has adhered to

(2) **No sharp, foreign objects, please.** Contrary to what you may have heard or read, it is dangerous to use a knife, screwdriver, or other instrument around the inside of a pot to loosen a plant for removal and potting on. This always rips and rends the tender root system, regardless of how carefully it is done. You may get away with it the first or second time, but the third time could spell disaster for a prized specimen. A plant that

won't release with conventional methods may be flooded out by successive irrigations, by forcing water from a hose up through the drainage hole, or by thumping its sides against a rigid surface. For larger specimens, try rolling it across a deck or patio, after tying up the foliage first to protect it. If none of these methods works, give some thought to sacrificing the container. The plant is probably worth more (intrinsically *and* extrinsically) than the container. Immerse the plant, pot and all, in a washtub or bucket of water for fifteen minutes, then take a hammer and strike the pot firmly just below the rim on opposing sides. The pot should crack and fall away.

(3) **A gentle touch means so much.** Plants are tender and fragile, and appreciate being handled delicately. One tempting form of mistreatment, however unintentional, that may occur to you as you're potting up a plant is to use its stem as a convenient handle to extricate it from its pot or move it around. This may be almost irresistible, but please resist it anyway. You may break the plant off at the soil line or rip away roots. It's comparable to someone helping you up from a fall by grabbing you by the throat.

Cut-Away View: Potting From the Nursery Can

1. Have nursery cut metal can. Transplant same day.
2. Prepare new pot ahead of time.
3. Water thoroughly with Vitamin B-1 solution.
4. Remove plant by grasping soil ball, not stem.
5. Center in new pot, fill with soil, tamp firmly.
6. Water thoroughly again.

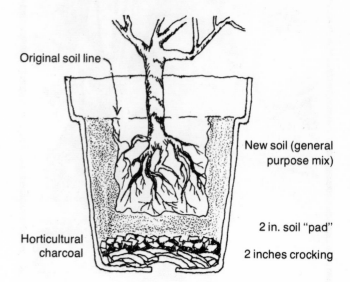

Original soil line

New soil (general purpose mix)

2 in. soil "pad"

2 inches crocking

Horticultural charcoal

Chapter 4

Basic Plant Care

You've got to know a little botany—at least the basics—if you want to grow bigger and better plants. If you loathed the life sciences in school, you'll find we've kept the material basic and easy to comprehend; if you were a straight-A science student, skim.

Plant requirements. Plants need three things to *survive* indoors: 1) LIGHT, 2) WATER, and 3) AIR. They require three additional things to *thrive* indoors: 1) HUMIDITY, 2) FERTILIZERS, and 3) LOVE. Let's explore each of these in turn.

LIGHT: Plants derive energy from light just as we do from the sun. Light is the trigger which sets into motion the complex process of photosynthesis (see glossary) which, simply stated, means the manufacturing of food for growth.

How much light do plants need? It varies from specimen to specimen. Some, such as the *Ficus decora* (rubber tree) and *Spathiphyllum*, can and do grow well in very dim light. Others like some sun, but most prefer bright-to-medium light (see illustration).

Some specimens that are not getting light of sufficient intensity take on a pale, chlorotic (yellowish) appearance, and some, such as the *Cissus rhombifolia* (grape ivy), turn pale if they're getting too much light. You'll find the light requirements of many specimens in the section on individual plant care.

WATER: It is rare that a novice gardener will kill a plant by withholding water; it's usually the other way around. Most beginners drench a plant daily, and few plants can handle that much water and survive.

Part of the problem is that most novices feel they are responsible for a plant's well-being, and they take this responsibility seriously. They feel they should be doing something to the plant every day to enhance its chances for survival and hasten its adjustment to its new surroundings. Instead of pouring quarts of water on their plant, they would have much greater success if they watered the plant about one day a week and talked to it the other six days.

Plants, of course, do need water, but they want it when they need it, not when we decide to give it. This is why, as your collection of specimens grows, you would be foolish to adopt a rigid watering schedule where you irrigate all your plants on a given day each week. While this may be convenient for you, it could be lethal to some of your plants.

How do you know when it's time to water? Some "experts" recommend watering when the top soil is dry. This can get you into trouble with your plants. The top soil is exposed to the warm interior air and dries out rapidly, but the soil further down is often adequately moist. This is

Light Intensities

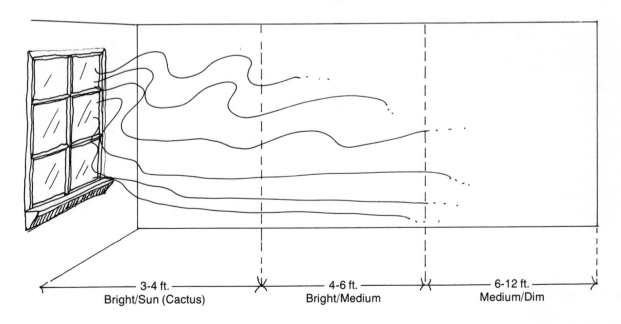

|←——— 3-4 ft. ———→|←——— 4-6 ft. ———→|←——— 6-12 ft. ———→|
Bright/Sun (Cactus) Bright/Medium Medium/Dim

especially true of a soil mixture which contains a lot of leaf mold or sand, which dries out on top in a matter of hours after you irrigate.

The most reliable test for determining the proper time to water almost all types of plants, and one that has been used by indoor gardeners for decades, is to insert your finger in the soil to the first knuckle. If the soil feels moist, don't water; if it's dry, water. There are exceptions to this guideline. Obviously, cacti and other succulents prefer their soil on the dry side. The *Crassula argentea* (jade tree) will usually start to "prune up" and drop leaves rapidly if it's watered oftener than every ten days, depending on its location in the home. Others, such as the *Chlorophytum comosum* (spider plant), flag and deteriorate if the soil is not kept continuously moist.

Victim of the Watering Can

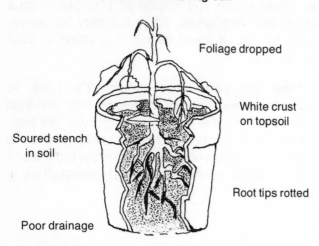

Foliage dropped

White crust on topsoil

Soured stench in soil

Root tips rotted

Poor drainage

It might be illuminating, at this point, to explain what happens when you irrigate a plant. As the water passes through the soil, it picks up nutrients (plant food) from the soil. The feeder roots absorb the water, and the leaves—which are being stimulated by light—pull the moisture up through the stem to the leaves, thereby nourishing the entire plant.

As the soil dries out over the next few days, tiny air pockets are formed in the spaces created by the shrinking soil particles. These air pockets are vital to a plant's well-being, for they provide the roots with the oxygen they need to thrive. The drying soil and oxygen stimulate the feeder roots to move around through the soil seeking moisture and food, and this exercise keeps the roots and the plant in top physical form. Now, if you break this

cycle by drowning the plant with too frequent waterings, the plant is almost invariably doomed. Continually wet soil rots the feeder roots, then the entire root structure, and ultimately the plant succumbs. You must provide a period of drought between irrigations if a plant is to survive.

There are exceptions to this rule, too. Certain specimens not only can take continuously damp (but not wet) conditions, but seem to require almost daily watering. Most plants, though, prefer a drink only every seven to ten days, on the average.

Some plants can and have adapted to daily drenching, but this is really a fool's game. Eventually this must lead to the destruction of the plant's root system. Some may say, as they have to us: "Oh, yeah? Well, I've been watering my dracaena every day for a year and it's doing great!" That's quite possible, for several reasons. (1) Plants are amazingly adaptable. They often overcome tremendous odds in their struggle for survival. (2) If a large-foliage plant is getting only a cup of water daily and is not being drenched, it often can cope with this since the water probably just barely reaches the feeder roots. (3) The location of the plant may be saving it from drowning. A bright, partially sunny window causes a plant to transpire (exude water vapor; see glossary) more rapidly and to pull a greater volume of water up from the soil. These are the primary reasons why an overwatered plant hangs in there month after month. The point is, why take a chance on killing the plant? Give it what it requires for good health—nothing more, nothing less.

Water types. The only water that shouldn't be used to irrigate your plants is artificially softened water. A plant's system gets indigestion, so to speak, from it and eventually will probably collapse. Rainwater is excellent, if you can get enough of it, but if you live in an area where air pollution is prevalent, eschew rainwater. Tapwater is fine, unless it is overloaded with chlorine, minerals, or other contaminants. If you can smell or taste chlorine in your tapwater, let it stand overnight so that the chlorine has a chance to evaporate. Minerals and other impurities will usually settle if the water is set aside for a few hours. Or to be on the safe side you can pour a half-inch layer of horticultural charcoal over the top soil of your plants. The charcoal will filter out nearly all impurities and help keep the soil "sweet" in the process.

If the water in your area simply isn't potable, and if nearly everyone in town drinks bottled or distilled water, better not give the tapwater to your plants either. Although it may raise your bottled water bill slightly, be magnanimous and give your foliage friends bottled water too. After all, they do a lot for you all year long and they rely on you totally for their well-being.

It is crucial for your plant's delicate systems that you bring the water to room temperature (tepid) before pouring it into the pot. Water that is too hot or too cold affects a plant the same way stepping into a hot or cold shower affects you—sudden shock. While we survive such minor shocks to our system, a plant often doesn't and collapses.

Which brings up another horticulturally dangerous fad that seems to be catching on. Almost monthly, one can find plant care articles in which the author gushes on and on breathlessly about what a clever way he or she has hit on to water plants. "I simply pour a tray of ice cubes on the top soil," the author writes, "and let them melt. This gives the plant a slow, gentle, natural drink, just like Mother Nature." It also can give a plant's subsurface roots a helluva shock and even freeze them. Many plants—most ferns, for example—are shallow-rooted and have their delicate root system spread out either on top of the top soil or just below its surface. It should be obvious that the freezing-thawing treatment is potentially lethal.

There is really no basis for the prevalent belief among some indoor gardeners that a sudden rush of water into the pot is harmful to a plant, provided it's tepid. Some plants, though, do prefer to be watered from the bottom—*Helxine soleirolii*, or Baby tears, for example—or by the old technique of double-pot watering (a smaller pot set inside a larger pot with the space between packed with sphagnum moss. The moss is watered and the moisture passes through the walls of the smaller pot), but these are in the minority.

As a matter of fact, most plants really *need* to have their soil saturated when you irrigate. You should water until you see moisture oozing out of the drainage hole each time, then give the plant only TLC until it's time to repeat the process. Shallow watering stimulates root growth in the upper two or three inches of the pot. Then, if the top soil is allowed to dry out and stay arid more than a few days, these roots die, and the plant must transfer

energy which would have been used in new foliage growth to developing new roots.

During spring and summer you should submerge the entire pot in a bucket of water at least every three or four weeks. This causes water to penetrate the entire soil ball, which almost never happens when you water in the conventional manner. The reason is simple. As the water filters down through the soil, it carves out little tunnels and the force of gravity takes over from there. Each time you irrigate, the water tends to rush down these tunnels and out the bottom, and it never reaches the rest of the soil ball. Periodically dunking the entire pot saturates the soil and usually collapses the eroded tunnels. After soaking the pot, let the plant go an extra four or five days before watering again. If, for example, you've found the plant needs water every eight or ten days, give it a drought period of thirteen to fifteen days.

After you've watered your plants, go back a few minutes later and make sure the bases of the pots are not submerged in water. Only a very few specimens take up water from the saucer; others will drown if left sitting in a swamp. Some water in the saucer is good, provided there are pebbles or other material to raise the base of the pot above the water level. (See illustration.) This creates a microclimate (see glossary), which gently bathes the foliage with rising waves of humid air.

Microclimate

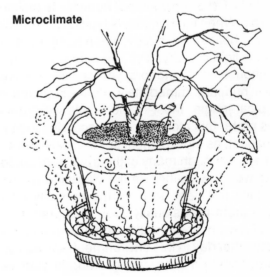

Rising water vapor raises humidity.

AIR: All plants prefer continuously-circulating fresh air, which provides them with the oxygen and moisture they need to carry out respiration. This is not so great a problem in spring and summer when you have the house opened up or have the air conditioning on, but in fall and winter, when the heater is kept running most of the day, fresh air is rare. The high heat burns up some of the oxygen and we breathe up some more, and what's left—if any—goes to the plants. Newer homes are designed with climate control that changes the air inside regularly, but older homes and most apartments have no such modern feature. Still, plants grown in these primitive environments somehow struggle through the winter.

Temperature. The temperature levels of pioneer homes were much better suited to most plants than those of our modern environments. Most of us feel comfortable in a room that is 78° to 82°. Plants, on the other hand—and this includes the tropicals—generally prefer a temperature range of 55° at night to 68° during the day, and many would do better with a minimum daytime temperature closer to 60°. We can get away with high temperatures by keeping the humidity high, but few of us are so concerned about our plants that we're willing to adjust our lifestyle to their preferences. Fortunately, most species are willing to adjust theirs to ours. With the new push from government for us to lower our thermostats to 68°, at least our plants will be much more comfortable and happier.

HUMIDITY: Simply stated, humidity is moisture in the air. When the humidity is high on a warm day, the air is heavy and muggy; when humidity is low, the air is light and dry. If you've ever walked into a greenhouse from outdoors, you can tell the difference in humidity immediately. It's like stepping into a tropical jungle. Most of the plants we grow indoors prefer this moist air, for it recreates their native habitat, as most of them are tropicals and subtropicals. Although many of the traditional outdoor plants we grow inside are not classified as tropicals, they still need to have the humidity raised around them occasionally. Not, of course, to the level of a warm greenhouse, because you couldn't live day after day in this environment—at least, not without finding mushrooms growing in your ears and moss sprouting on the north side of your nose.

Water-covered pebbles in a plant's saucer is helpful for raising the humidity around that particular plant, as we've described, but as your collection grows, you need to cover a greater area. You can get very professional and purchase an expensive humidifier that automatically maintains a selected moisture level in the air. Then there are the less expensive room vaporizers which you can fill with water. O·· you can buy, for two dollars, a hand atomizer ., d mist your plants by hand, preferably once a day.

If you use the hand mister, which incidentally is quite effective and adequate in a limited area and time, be sure you cover with newspapers all wood floors, furniture and anything else which would suffer permanent damage from drifting mist and water spots. You should understand that the water drops don't simply sit on the leaves and evaporate; the plant's foliage absorbs some of the moisture through hundreds of tiny pores (stomata; see glossary).

Misting or syringing is beneficial in clearing these pores of dust, smoke residue from cooking and tobacco, etc., so the plant can breathe. You can do the job in the bathtub or shower stall with a gentle, tepid spray or outside on mild days with a hose.

Plants that have been inside all winter, or whose leaves have been "enhanced" by one of the leaf shine products, should first be gently washed with lukewarm water and a bar of Ivory soap suds (cover the pot and soil with aluminum foil before you begin), then thoroughly rinsed with clear water to remove the soap residue. This not only unblocks a plant's "sinuses," it also helps eradicate and/or discourage pests, which will be covered in an ensuing chapter.

Another technique for raising the humidity that works well is to place pots, pans, or other containers of steaming hot water under your large foliage plants. The rising moist air is appreciated by nearly all specimens and causes them to perk up noticeably almost immediately. You can't overdo this. The oftener you do it, the better your plants like it.

FERTILIZERS: Since we've snatched plants from the bosom of Mother Nature, who provides them with the "milk of life" to sustain them, we must wet nurse the little tykes the rest of their lives. Plants need nitrogen, phosphorous, and potash, as well as the trace elements calcium, magnesium, sulphur, iron, manganese, boron, copper, and zinc to grow well and stay healthy.

You needn't worry about fertilizer for the first four to six months after you've acquired a plant.

The commercial grower has added enough fertilizer to carry the plant at least half a year before he delivered it to the nursery. If the end of the six-month period comes in the fall or winter, hold off feeding until spring. The plant can't use the extra nutrition until it has begun to grow again, and if you add food, you may kill it by loading the soil with mineral salts.

What is fertilizer? It can be compared to vitamins in the human system. We need extra nutritional help if we are not eating well-balanced meals consistently. This nutritional booster is taken in the form of vitamins. When plants use up the nutrients in the soil, they need "vitamins," too, available in the form of plant foods or fertilizers. There are two kinds of fertilizers: *organics*, whose sources are decomposed fish, manures, leaves and other once-living matter; and *chemical*, which are concentrated mineral salts.

A *complete* fertilizer has the three major food elements plants must have to live and thrive: nitrogen, phosphorous and potassium, or potash. These are usually listed on the label by their percentages: for example, 10-5-5, which means 10% nitrogen, 5% phosphorous, and 5% potassium. These elements are always listed in the same order. Sometimes the elements are simply shown by their chemical symbols: N (nitrogen), P (phosphorous), and K (potassium).

5% Nitrogen
10% Phosphorous
5% Potash

What fertilizer does. Nitrogen encourages leaf development and plant growth; phosphorous or phosphate causes healthy and vigorous root development and helps a plant mature rapidly; and potassium also contributes to root growth and makes stems strong and sturdy.

Every plant-lover has his or her favorite fertilizer. Through the process of elimination, we've narrowed the list down to three we rely on. They work for us, but you may have better success with others. First of all, for a gentle, slow-acting plant food, we like several different brands of fish emulsion (but only the ones containing chelated iron). For a stronger, faster-acting nutritional program, we prefer Stern's "Miracle-Gro" (15-30-15). It also contains chelated iron, as does the other Stern product which works well for acid-loving plants, "Miracid" (30-10-10).

All the fertilizers we use are water soluble. We've found these are easiest to use, and because they are completely dissolved in water, the nutrients are readily available to the plant. You can also use dry fertilizers, which are scratched into the topsoil and watered in, or the plant tablets or pellets which are designed to dissolve over a period of days and nourish the plant more slowly.

Dry fertilizers are, from our viewpoint, more troublesome and unsightly, with the exception of *bonemeal*, which is a very gentle, non-burning fertilizer. It breaks down extremely slowly and is often recommended, for that reason, to over-zealous novices who are usually prone to overdo everything horticultural until they've learned better. The problem with bonemeal is that it must go in the bottom layer of soil in the pot. If you try to scratch it in the top soil, it'll just sit there interminably. If you do succeed in getting it worked down into the soil, you've really got trouble. The feeder roots will start growing up to the bonemeal, instead of down and out of harm's way.

While, admittedly, fertilizer is important in the culture of beautiful and healthy plants, it is highly overrated as a cureall for plant ailments and a stimulant to increased growth and size. There is a tendency among some pretty knowledgeable plant lovers to give their plants a dose of plant food at the first sign of a brown tip or temporary cessation of growth. Others are out to grow freaks of nature, producing gigantism in every specimen they own. If their collections are thriving as a result, well and good. But don't let their enthusiasm infect you.

First of all, a plant is seldom perfect, even in a greenhouse where conditions are ideal. An occasional brown tip or the loss of one or two leaves are natural phenomena in plant culture. They don't mean the plant is nutritionally deficient. Second, a plant that has slowed or entirely stopped all visible growth is probably just sacking out for a few weeks. This, too, is normal and is called *dormancy*. Most plants have (or need) a period of rest and it usually comes in the winter months. That's why you should withhold *all* fertilizer from fall to spring (and cut back on water, also). Plants need this period of inactivity to rejuvenate and revitalize their systems for their vigorous growth period in spring and summer. If you deprive them of their "vacation," they'll go on strike next spring and put out, perhaps, only a few feeble leaves. Or worse, the heavy concentration of fertilizer in the soil will burn the plant.

Fertilizer *burn* is the result of excess mineral salts in the soil. The root hairs lose moisture and the tissue begins to deteriorate. For this reason, it's a good idea to saturate the soil of any plant you buy with water to dissolve salts that may have accumulated, and fifteen to thirty minutes later, to flush the salts out of the pot or can by successive drenchings.

When you do feed your plants, avoid the temptation to over-feed. We always dilute 50% *more* than the label recommends, then feed twice as often, just to play it safe. It is crucial, also, that the soil be moist when you fertilize to prevent root burn. Simply water normally, wait a few minutes, then add the fertilizer solution.

LOVE: Well, love isn't something you usually learn in Botany 1-A or Principles of Biology (unless a classmate of the opposite sex is stirring up your hormones), but plants thrive better if you share your affection with them. We find it difficult to be just "fond of" plants—we *love* them. They know it and return it by growing up nice and cute.

How do you "love" a plant? First of all, you never think or say mean things to it. Yes, plants are sensitive even to your thoughts. Plants are living entities, just as we are. Why shouldn't we be able to establish rapport with them? Second, talk *to* your plants, not *at* them. Some of our friends probably think we're candidates for the funny farm when they hear us talking to ours. We don't bore them with mundane prattle, or baby-talk them, or scare them with news from the front page of the paper. We simply inquire about their health and tell them how beautiful they are. They're really suckers for subtle flattery. Third, we play music for them. Some lab experiments have shown that plants are music-lovers, preferring classical music. They are not at all fond of hard rock. It makes them neurotic, according to the scientists. We give our plants a few hours a day of Vivaldi, Bach, and Handel. They like the baroque sounds, especially concertos for strings. If we're going to be gone for a day or two, we leave on our local classical, non-commercial radio station to keep them company.

The other things we do to communicate our affection are largely good horticultural practices: no over-feeding or over-watering; leaves kept dust-free; regular physical checkups to make certain no bugs have sneaked up when they weren't looking; regular annual root-checks to make sure there's ample room to roam. There you have it.

And there you have basic plant care. That wasn't all that painful, was it? If you follow these few simple guidelines, you should have resounding success as an indoor gardener.

Chapter 5

Soils & Conditioners

Soil composition for your plants is important, but not all that critical to their well-being. Plants can grow in virtually any planting medium that will hold water and nutrients. Your goal for optimum results, however, should be a rich, well-draining composition that more or less duplicates the soil characteristics of the plant's place of origin.

General purpose soil for tropicals and sub-tropicals. As a general rule, nearly all foliage jungle and rainforest plants—which includes 80% of the plants most of us grow—thrive in a slightly acid soil that drains well, yet retains some moisture to fulfill water requirements over a period of days. Ideally the formula will contain rich top *soil*; *leaf mold* (decayed leaves, branches, and bark); *peat moss*; coarse, sharp builders' *sand* (to promote good drainage); horticultural *charcoal*; and, perhaps, some *bonemeal*.

There are dozens of packaged soil mixes on the market formulated for tropicals which claim to be "ready-to-use," but most require some additional ingredients to give them body. Some are primarily bark and/or leaf mold and are too light, others are mostly sand, and still others are heavy on the peat moss. The one which comes closest to our requirements is "Supersoil," but we usually end up adding leaf mold to give it a coarser texture and greater body.

Soil and soil amendments. Let's examine the ideal soil recipe and see what the various ingredients contribute to plant health. First of all, the soil contains the nutrients and trace elements the plant needs. Leaf mold is rich in nutrients and holds moisture; the bits of bark and stems it contains give a plant's roots a stable anchor. Peat moss has nutrient value, but its primary contribution is its moisture-holding capability. Peat moss must first be shredded, then soaked with hot water before using. It should never go into the potting mix dry or it will never absorb water. Builders' sand helps hold the soil open, thereby encouraging good drainage. Beach sand is too fine and packs down. About the only source of sharp builders' sand is a building-supply outlet that sells cement. Some thoughtful nurserymen have begun to stock it. Horticultural charcoal has a two-fold purpose: until it decomposes, it helps open up the soil, and it also keeps the soil from souring; bonemeal, as we've seen, is an organic source of slow-acting phosphate, and is an optional ingredient.

All of these additives are termed *amendments*, since they introduce changes into the characteristics of the potting soil. There are other amendments which are used in addition to, or in place of, some of the foregoing. Some of these are *perlite* which is a white, porous rock of volcanic origin. It is often used by growers to improve moisture retention and promote better aeration of their potting medium. Our objection to perlite is purely subjective—it's not very attractive when it's visible in the top soil, but this can be obviated by eliminating it from the top layer of soil when you're potting up. *Vermiculite*, which is a mineral mica that has been expanded by heat to enhance its water-holding capacity, is another popular conditioner. It can hold eight to ten times its weight in water. It shares the same feature of unattractiveness with perlite and can be treated in the same way when potting. Other amendments often used are *pumice, sawdust, coal cinders* and ground *bark*.

What about garden soil? Yes, you can use it, if you must, but only after treatment. Soil from the garden presents some problems which, in our opinion, make it more trouble than it's worth. However, if you have no convenient source of pasteurized and packaged potting mix, garden soil may be your only choice. Some of the problems are: contamination with weed, grass, and flower seeds which will germinate if not treated; a heavy concentration of strong fertilizers which are much too harsh for most delicate tropicals; probable infestation with soil-borne grubs and other destructive insects, which will be delighted to move inside where it's warm and even more ecstatic with the tasty meal of your prized specimens; and, especially in gardens where vegetables have been grown in successive years, there may be present dormant damp-off fungi which can damage or destroy your plants.

You can eliminate most of these problems and make garden soil relatively safe by baking it in your oven. Simply line a pan with aluminum foil, or make a pan from heavy-duty foil, pour in a layer no deeper than two inches, add a cup and a half of water, and bake for an hour at about 215°. Avoid overdoing it by extending the time or raising the temperature. If you do, microorganisms that enhance soil fertility may be killed along with the pests and seeds. Proper treatment, though, improves soil fertility.

Baking soil creates an odor problem. If there are delicate, sensitive noses in your household, use another technique which is just as effective. Pour the soil in a turkey-size plastic "brown-in" bag, add a cup of water, seal, and place on a cookie sheet. This technique eliminates the odor problem. You should extend the baking time an additional fifteen minutes with the bag approach.

Don't forget to add water, whichever method you use. Soil that is baked dry comes out like fine powder and is almost impossible to handle.

Garden soil still requires some amendments to make it suitable for use. In most cases, garden soil is what is called "loam," which can be loosely defined as sandy soil, so you can usually eliminate sand as an additive. Some leaf mold and charcoal should make it just about right as a general-purpose mix.

Basic Soil Recipe
(General purpose use)

2 parts pasteurized soil

1 part leaf mold

1 part shredded (and soaked) peat moss

½ cup horticultural charcoal to each gallon of soil mix

2 tablespoons of steamed bonemeal (mixed in base layer of soil in pot)

Add to this:

1 cup coarse, sharp sand or gravel to each gallon of soil mix

Acid soils. Determining the acidity or alkalinity of the soil can get complex and is usually much more technical than most plant-lovers want to get. It involves the pH scale (hydrogen ion concentration), which runs from one to fourteen. A pH of seven is neutral and means that the soil is evenly balanced between acidity and alkalinity. Readings above seven indicate alkalinity, or "sweetness"; readings below seven indicate acidity, or "sourness." Soils which contain a greater proportion of acid-bearing materials (such as peat moss, oak and pine leaf mold, or rotted hardwood sawdust) rather than loam are acid soils.

Indoor gardeners seldom have a need to worry about the pH factor of their soil. The plants which require acidity can be accommodated simply by adding acid amendments to the potting mix. Some of the plants which prefer acid soil are amaryllis, azalea, dieffenbachia, most ferns and philodendrons, and sheffleras.

Acid Soil Recipe

5 parts coarse (shredded) peat moss

2 parts oak leaf mold

1 part pasteurized soil

1 part sand (coarse, sharp) or gravel

Fast-draining soils. Virtually all cacti and most other succulents thrive in specially formulated soil recipes with the accent on quick evacuation of excess water immediately after irrigation. Succulence means "water-storing." When you water a cactus or other succulent, the plant takes up the water it needs and stores it in its tissues. Once this is done, the plant has all the moisture it wants and will rot if its soil retains moisture over a period of days. This is why the soil must be formulated to shed water rapidly. Parenthetically, you should also know that cacti should only be watered on sunny days, and if possible, only when the plants are sitting directly in the sun. The sun's rays help the cacti pull up the water from the soil and throw off the excess through transpiration.

Fast-Draining Soil Recipe
Desert-type cacti

1 part coarse, sharp builders' sand or gravel

1 part sandy soil

1 part limestone

Other succulents

1 part coarse sand or gravel

1 part peat moss or ground bark

1 part pasteurized soil

2 tablespoons of steamed bonemeal (Optional)

SPECIAL NOTE: All soil eventually gets old and breaks down. After a few years, it has probably absorbed an excessive amount of undissolved mineral salts (fertilizer residue) which can be harmful to a plant. Annual top dressing—replacing the first two inches or so of soil in the pot—helps prolong a soil's fertility, but eventually the continuous demands by the plant, loss of aeration by packing down into hardpan from week after week of watering, and the fertilizer build-up all take too great a toll. Inevitably, the plant must be re-potted in fresh, virgin soil if it is to continue to thrive.

Chapter 6

Propagating Plants Shrubs & Trees

Sooner or later, as a confirmed plant lover and collector, you'll be tempted to try "growing your own" from seed, cuttings, air layering, root division, or rooting offsets and runners. Some of these propagation techniques are difficult, fraught with failures, and demand uncommon patience; others are easy, virtually guaranteed of success, and produce almost immediate results. To really get into plant cultivation, though, you should try them all eventually. There is immense satisfaction in knowing that you grew a thriving, healthy plant from a tiny seed or piece of stem, just like the professionals, but without their expensively equipped greenhouses.

The two basic methods of propagation are called *sexual*, which is propagation by seed, and *asexual* or *vegetative*, which means that a part of the plant's vegetation is used instead of seed.

Sexual propagation. Of the two techniques, seed propagation is both the most satisfying and the most frustrating. On the one hand, if you are successful in bringing a plant to maturity from seed, you can mentally pat yourself on the back for a superlative achievement in the face of tremendous odds. On the other hand, the many months of coddling and anxiety, not to mention the long wait (sometimes years) for impressive results, make propagation from seed an undertaking for those who can take frequent failures in stride and have the undiminished patience of a Luther Burbank.

Some of the many plants which can successfully be grown from seed by those with only basic horticultural knowledge and equipment are abutilon, asparagus fern (*A. sprengerii*), bird of paradise (*Strelitzia reginae*), rubber tree (*Ficus decora elastica*), fuchsia, podocarpus, pomegranate (*Punica granatum*) and silk oak (*Grevillea robusta*).

There are several guidelines to follow when you propagate from seeds that will enhance your chances for probable success. First of all, start with fresh seeds. All seeds you purchase from catalogs, nurseries, and garden centers have an expiration or planting season date stamped on one end of the packet. Seeds that are outdated or are from a previous growing season may not germinate, and you will have wasted a lot of time.

If you're using seeds you've harvested from your own plants, they are usually ripe and ready to plant when they've turned brown. Don't pluck them green or they probably won't germinate since they haven't completed their maturation cycle. Almost all seeds germinate faster if they're soaked overnight in warm water, but those which are fine and look like powder should not be immersed in water, for obvious reasons. Usually, the seedsman states on the packet whether the seeds should be soaked before planting. In the absence of instructions, go ahead and soak.

Planting nurseries. Professional growers sow in large flats either of wood or plastic, but apple crates, shallow bulb pans, cake or loaf pans, coffee cans or virtually any other container which will hold planting media works just as well for germinating seeds. The success or failure of propagating from seeds is seldom determined by the materials or facilities one has at his or her disposal, but rather in the techniques used. Prepare the container by punching holes in the bottom for good drainage or by dry welling with an inch or two of rocks, pebbles or clay shards. Fruit crates may be lined with newspaper or plastic, then a layer of sphagnum moss added to keep the potting medium from sifting through the gaps in the crates.

Seed Propagation

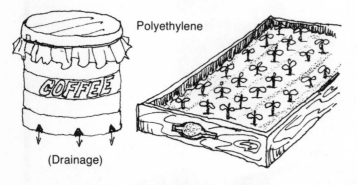

Polyethylene

COFFEE

(Drainage)

Some thought, obviously, must be given to moisture leakage through drainage holes. The easiest way to deal with this problem is setting a cookie sheet (with raised sides all around) under the pots or pans to catch the excess water. The Teflon-coated types don't rust but cost a few cents more.

Before adding your potting medium, put a layer of crocking one to two inches deep in the bottom, as you would if you were potting up a mature plant, and for the same reason.

Planting seeds. It isn't necessary to cover small seeds—they have a knack for settling into the planting medium naturally. Very fine, dust-like seeds would be difficult to "plant" anyway. Just sprinkle them on the top. Larger seeds should be buried just under the top soil, but follow packet directions for precise instructions, unless you've harvested your own.

For the various fruit seeds and pits, a depth of an inch usually is sufficient to induce germination, but your local nurseryman can give you the best guideline on planting depths. Avocado seeds started in soil should only be buried (large end down) to three-quarters of their depth. If you cover the entire seed, nine times out of ten, it won't germinate.

Seeds need four things to germinate and thrive: moisture, light, moderate heat, and occasional ventilation.

Moisture / humidity. The first requirement, moisture, is a critical factor. The seeds must be surrounded by moisture, but not floating in a swamp. This is where the potting or seed-bed medium comes in. You need a planting medium which will hold the precise amount of moisture needed through the germination process.

Many horticulturalists, amateur and professional, swear by *milled sphagnum moss*, which is available at your garden center, because it eliminates the problem of damp-off fungus which, in unpasteurized soil, kills young seedlings. Others swear at it because it often "crusts over." Still others use *peat moss, perlite* or *vermiculite*, either singly or in combination. Cornell University has developed a popular planting material which is marketed under the trade name, "Peat-Lite." This, also, should be universally available.

In our experience, one of the best and virtually fool-proof of all the planting media for everything but cacti and other succulents is one composed of equal parts milled sphagnum moss and perlite. You can buy both ingredients almost everywhere and mix them yourself in a fifty-fifty proportion. For cacti and succulents, add sand to the mix.

Soil, whether packaged and pasteurized or baked garden loam, as a seeding medium must be watched carefully. It has a tendency to become boggy, or—more often—to dry out rapidly and ruin all your preparations and hopes. Untreated soil should never be used for seed germination. It usually carries destructive damp-off fungus organisms which cause seedlings to wilt and die at the soil line.

While seeds are germinating and growing into seedlings, they require a microclimate, or environment within an environment, of high humidity. The least expensive way to provide this when using makeshift containers such as coffee cans, terrarium or aquarium tanks, or the like, is that miracle of twentieth century technology, polyethylene plastic wrap. Most brands can be affixed to the top of any container simply by pressing it into place or holding it with rubber bands. Glass works as well as a cover, but is more expensive. Materials that aren't transparent should be used only until the seedlings appear, since they cut down on the intensity of light, which would hamper seedling growth.

Light is important after the seeds have germinated and become seedlings. For thick, bushy growth, provide very bright illumination, but no direct sun, which will cook the young plants to death or at least give them heat prostration. Too little light encourages leggy growth. The seedlings should be rotated two or three times a week to keep them from becoming permanently sway-backed from reaching for light. In fact, *all* plants should be given a half turn weekly if they're positioned near or in front of a window, to keep them growing straight.

Heat. Seeds need moderate heat to germinate, but once they've developed into seedlings, you'll get better growth by keeping the plantlets cool. A spot near a radiator or heating vent may supply adequate heat for germination, but the seeds are then subject to the vagaries of a thermostat. A more precise way of providing consistent warmth at the ideal level is to purchase, for about $4.95, low-watt electric cables which are made for heating seed flats. These work most efficiently if you're planting in apple crates or regular seed flats.

Ventilation. Continuously damp, stagnant air promotes the development of fungus and mold, especially in soil, so covered flats should be aired for a few minutes every day. If polyethylene is used as a cover, a few holes poked through it with a sharp pencil usually eliminates the need for daily ventilation. This also encourages greater moisture evaporation and thus requires more attention on your part to ensure against excessive drying of the planting medium.

Fertilizing and thinning. After seedlings have developed two distinct pairs of leaves, they should be thinned out. Only those seedlings which seem to be thriving well (usually the tallest) should be kept for growing on, particularly if you only want to propagate a few plants. Thinning will produce stronger, healthier plants since the remaining seedlings don't have to compete for survival.

Thinned-out plants can be transplanted into 1¼-inch terra cotta pots and set in a covered terrarium or aquarium tank. Until they are further along, they still need high humidity. Now you should start feeding the seedlings with a weak solution (quarter strength) of fertilizer about every third week, or follow directions on the seed packet.

Asexual (vegetative) propagation, as we have seen, involves utilizing a part or offset of a mature plant. It is also the technique used in those cases where seed propagation is difficult or impossible to achieve.

Runners and suckers. Of all the vegetative propagation techniques, rooting runners and suckers is probably the easiest. Unfortunately, it is also the least applicable, since only a few plants produce runners and suckers. The spider plant (*Chlorophytum comosum*) is the most common example of a runner-producer. These are miniature replicas of the mother plant and are simply rooted in a smaller pot while still attached by their umbilical cord (see illustrations) by anchoring them to the top soil with hairpins. They root so easily, they can even be cut from the main plant before rooting and then potted up.

Some of the plants which produce offsets or suckers are *Cordyline stricta*, screwpine (*Pandanus veitchii*) and such succulents as echeveria, agave, and aloe. Simply cut away the sucker close to the main plant, and if they are potted up in the soil recipe they require, they usually develop root structures of their own. An alternative method which has proved successful is to insert the suckers in sharp, coarse sand that is kept continually moist until they've developed roots, then pot them up in the proper soil formulation.

Cuttings. A fast propagation method is taking cuttings from mature plants and inducing them to root. Softwood cuttings—those from green stems—are easiest; hardwood cuttings—those from tough, woody stems characteristic of such plants as aralia, dracaena and podocarpus—are

This spider plant has produced two runners which have been rooted in smaller pots.

After rooting has been accomplished, plantlets are cut from mother plant and now where there was one, there are three.

the most difficult and are better candidates for air layering, which we'll explore a little further on. Three species which respond particularly well to cutting propagation are azalea, mahonia, and yew.

The best time to take cuttings is in the spring, when most plants have entered their active growth period. Select your cutting from new, green growth by making a clean diagonal cut just below a node, or joint, in the branch. Dip the cut end in hormone rooting powder, which will encourage faster root development and discourage decay, place the cutting immediately in the rooting medium, and water well.

Rooting media for cuttings. The most frequently used rooting medium for softwood and hardwood cuttings is a fifty-fifty mixture of coarse sand and peat moss; for cacti and other succulents, sand alone is ideal, since it doesn't hold water which can rot those water-storing species. Other rooting media are sphagnum moss, vermiculite, and perlite, which can be used singly or in combination.

Root development time for cuttings varies widely between species. Ivies often root in a mere ten days, while some of the woody-stemmed varieties may require as long as two months. Contrary to what you may have read or heard, you may gently pull cuttings up once a week to check for root development without hampering their progress or

harming them. When roots are about an inch long, you should move the cuttings to small individual pots and stake them until their roots are capable of supporting the top growth. Remember to maintain the same depth in the new container as in the rooting medium; never allow the soil to rise higher on the stem or a plant will rot, and never let it sink lower or the roots will dry out and die.

Cuttings require high humidity to prevent wilt. The leaf surfaces continue to transpire (throw off) moisture, but they don't have the root development yet to absorb and replace the moisture they've lost through evaporation. As with seedlings, you must create a high-humidity microclimate. An old aquarium tank to set the cuttings in is ideal for the purpose. If you don't have one, simply cover the pot or container with a plastic bag secured with rubber bands to the rim of the container. Keep the plastic from touching the foliage by inserting sticks or something similar around the inside rim of the pot to create a plastic tent. The moisture which is thrown off by the plant collects inside the tent and drips back in a continuous recycling effect. Set the container in bright light (no sun) for warmth and to encourage rapid, vigorous growth. The best temperature range for rooting is 70° to 80°.

Division. There are several plants which produce more than one stem from the soil line—cast-iron plant (*aspidistra*), spider plant (*Chlorophytum*

All will continue to produce runners.

1. Cutting in fresh water.   2. Ten to 14 days.

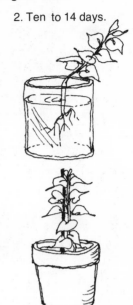

3. Two to three weeks.   4. Pot up and stake.

comosum), and most ferns. These additional stems can, with a very few exceptions, be divided to create two, three, or more plants; or they may be left to produce a fuller, larger plant. If you do decide to divide, it is best to do so in the spring to give both the donor and the divided plants a good chance to recover before their vigorous growth slows in late summer and fall.

First water the plant the day before with a Vitamin B-1 solution, to prevent transplant shock. Then knock the plant out of its pot and gently remove most of the soil from the roots. Some recommend breaking the plants and roots apart with one's bare hands or hacking them apart with a hatchet or cleaver. Our approach is more surgical. We sterilize a sharp butcher knife which is reserved for horticultural chores (and sterilized with antiseptic before storing) by holding it in a flame for thirty

seconds, letting it cool, then wiping off the black carbon deposit with a sterile cotton ball. We then lay the plant on its side and make a clean cut at a point which leaves most of the root ball with the donor plant, taking only enough root structure to sustain the divided plant.

Once the plants have been divided, re-pot immediately to prevent excessive drying of the roots and then water well. Let the newly divided plants almost dry out before irrigating again to encourage new root development.

Air layering. This is the ideal propagation technique for the hardwood, large-foliage specimens, such as croton, rubber tree (*Ficus elastica*), umbrella tree (*Shefflera*) and the like. Because of their large leaf surfaces, they often fail as cuttings because they dehydrate before roots can form, even with the provision of high humidity.

Rooting succulent stem/leaf cuttings in sand

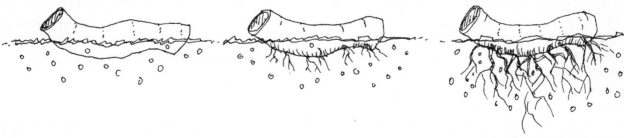

One week   Two weeks   Three weeks

Air Layering

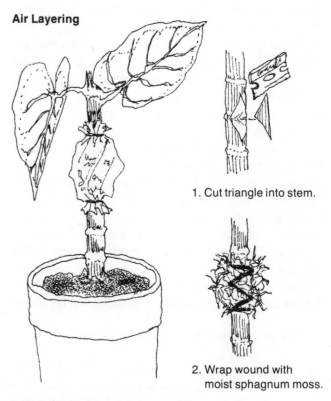

1. Cut triangle into stem.

2. Wrap wound with moist sphagnum moss.

3. Wrap and secure plastic wrap "cocoon."

The typical air-layering method involves taking a triangular piece of the stem from a point where you would like to induce roots to develop (see illustrations). In rubber trees, which usually drop their lower leaves rapidly from overwatering and begin to look spindly and leggy, this point is normally four to six inches below the lowest leaf. The cut is then packed with moist (never sopping wet) sphagnum moss which is packed tightly against the wound by twist-ties or cord, then the area is wrapped in an air-tight cocoon of plastic wrap which is sealed off, top and bottom, either with twist-ties or plastic tape.

Other techniques which achieve the same results include stripping away a one-inch band of bark all the way around the stem, or making an upward-slanting cut one third of the way through the stem, then inserting a piece of wooden match

One of the fastest methods of propagation is from cuttings of mature plants.

or a pebble in the wound to keep it from healing. In both methods, the area is packed with moss and wrapped, as described in the preceding paragraph. As with most propagating techniques, air layering is most productive in spring.

Air layering often involves a long wait—sometimes up to eight months with certain species. Most, however, are ready to separate from the donor plant in about two months. When you see roots filling the plastic wrap, you may cut off the air-layered section and pot it up. Stake it for support. The donor plant will probably begin immediately to stump-sprout, so now you'll have two small, full plants, instead of one tall, leggy plant.

What if you don't see roots in the plastic film, even after patiently waiting two months or longer? Well, this occasionally happens and is almost always the result of two things: 1) the cut wasn't deep enough, or 2) the moss dried out and the wound healed. In the first instance, you can rectify the problem by making a deeper cut. In the second case, you'll need to make a new cut and repack with damp moss. In the latter instance, make certain this time your plastic seal is air-tight. Check it every couple of weeks. If the moss dries out, moisten again and re-seal.

Chapter 7

Plant Parasites & Plant Maladies

Many people talk to their plants, but few people "listen" to them. Your plants are trying to tell you something when they begin to flag, yellow off, brown off, drop leaves, curl up, or totally collapse. What they're trying to say is, "HELP!"

Plant parasites. If you have adopted good horticultural procedures, the chances are that what may be wrong with your ailing green friend is something over which you have little control, at least initially—an invasion of parasites. But if you're an observant gardener, responsive to the needs and afflictions of your plants, you'll be aware, before it's too late, that unwelcome company has come to call on your collection.

Regardless of how observant and careful you are, plant pests often appear without warning. Some may have hitched a ride from the nursery or plant shop as eggs nestled snugly in the foliage. Others may be soil-borne, hiding among the roots. When the plant is brought indoors, the warm interior atmosphere creates an ideal nursery and breeding ground for them.

Unless a plant is severely infested, and this is highly unlikely unless you are a callous and indifferent gardener, you can cope with all of the pests successfully, with a little patience.

Most parasites which attack houseplants are sucking insects, including aphids, mealy bugs, red spider mites, scales, and white flies. The most common of these are mealy bugs and mites. All do their damage by sucking the sap, and hence the vitality, from a plant's stem and leaves, unlike chewing insects, which destroy or defoliate a plant by consuming stems and foliage.

Pesticide or organic controls? We Americans have always prided ourselves on our inventiveness, thoroughness, and dedication to performing a task to the best of our ability and technology. ("If a thing's worth doing, it's worth doing right!") We've brought this American Way to the problem of coping with garden pests to the point of overkill. We dump gallons of pesticide on our gardens at the first sign of a caterpillar or beetle.

We are two of the growing legion of nature lovers who are foursquare against the use of pesticides. We have all seen the effects of our past transgressions with the deadliest of all pesticides, DDT. We now know the damage we've done to the ecosystem by its use from World War II on. Crabs and fish have completely died out in many rivers and streams where they've lived and provided us with food for generations. All over the globe, animal and bird species are being decimated because of concentrations of DDT in their systems, and things are getting worse. Cancer in humans has even been linked to DDT (see "The Doomsday Book," by Gordon Rattray Taylor, pp. 134-135).

We simply don't need DDT and the other persistent chlorinated hydrocarbons (aldrin, chlordane, dieldrin, endrin, heptachlor, TDE, and toxaphene) which build up in the soil and get into the food chain, where they are passed on from the lowest life forms to humans. Mother Nature has been patient, but one suspects she's just about had it with us. We feel any plant infested seriously enough to require spraying with a pesticide or insecticide bomb should be discarded. Why? Let's take a hypothetical situation. Let's say you have a plant infested with red spider mites. You take it outside and spray it with a toxic "bug bomb." The spray drifts through the air and lands on some flowers. A bee comes along and picks up the pesticide and dies. A beneficial insect, such as a ladybug which feeds on aphids, also is contaminated. A bird eats the ladybug and passes the poison on to her offspring in her eggs.

Okay, that's not so serious, you may say. Well, add your pesticide to your neighbors', who may be using something much stronger and in much greater volume on their trees and flowers. And what about the people on the next block and the next? You begin to see the potential effect when you realize how much poison is being pumped into the soil and air. And this doesn't include the vast amounts of pollution from industrial and automotive wastes or the hundreds of gallons of insecticide mist from agricultural pest control programs which is often airborne for miles before it settles.

Pesticides aren't selective. They kill beneficial as well as destructive insects. We've already upset the balance of nature by decimating the natural enemies of predatory insects. There's even incontrovertible proof now that most harmful insects which are plaguing us today are immune to our strongest pesticides, and some are even *addicted* to them. If we don't stop soon, we may have the sterile planet we've been promised by the science fiction writers, a planet devoid of butterflies and bees, as well as locusts and weevils.

There are two alternatives to the deadly pesticides—organic controls and a few safe and/or degradable poisons which can be used as soil additives then watered in. These are the cures and treatments we'll explore.

Isolate ailing plants. At the first sign of insect infestation or fungus disease, isolate the plant immediately and begin treatment. Leaving the plant near (or worse, touching) other plants in your collection is flirting with disaster. All plant pests, with the exception of slow-moving scale, can move easily from one plant to the next, and in a matter of hours you can have a real emergency on your hands.

Systemic treatment for "hard cases." Sucking insects which seem immune to your organic assaults on them, or which return a few weeks after treatment, can be eradicated by one of the systemic poisons, such as Ortho's "Isotox." A systemic poison is absorbed by the roots and translocated through a plant's tissues. Shortly after a sucking insect extracts the systemically treated sap from any part of the plant, it dies. Most manufacturers of systemics recommend repeating the treatment in two weeks, to take care of newborn generations which may have hatched after the initial dosing. We've found one treatment is usually sufficient and protects the plant for at least a year.

Use a systemic poison in granular form. It's easier and safer. You simply scratch a circular "trench" in the top soil, completely encircling the plant, sprinkle in the recommended dosage, fill in the trench and tamp down, and water thoroughly to dissolve the granules and start the treatment. When you water, do so by letting the stream trickle down the stem and spread out gently over the top soil. This prevents washing the granules to the surface. Once the granules are wet they emit a sinister and unpleasant odor which is minimized if they're buried under an inch of top soil.

A word of caution. If you have small children, don't use *any* poisons in your plants. Most toddlers are quite fond of dirt, as you well know if you have tykes, and will consume great quantities as often as possible, if they are left to their own devices. The systemics are deadly poisons. When you use them, wear cheap gloves you can discard afterwards (paint stores sell cotton and plastic "one-shot" gloves for under fifty cents), and a plastic spoon for measuring. When you're finished, break the spoon in half and discard it to prevent its

use by someone else (particularly children) who isn't aware of its deadly residue. Don't smoke or eat while you're using these poisons. Wash (don't just rinse) with soap and water before smoking or eating. Finally, store any poisons safely out of reach of probing little fingers. You'd be amazed at the number of people who think the cabinet under the sink is sufficiently safe; it's the first place most kids are attracted to.

Coping with the "bug." **Mealy bugs** are, in our experience, the easiest of all the predators to see, recognize, and deal with. They are small, white insects which resemble tiny puffs of cotton. Like most pests, they favor the underside of leaves, deep crevices in foliage, and the axils. Because mealy bugs are so prolific, immediate action is called for, if you're to succeed in eradicating them.

Treatment: 1) If you've only a few, the easiest treatment is to dip a cotton swab in a little alcohol (or gin) and remove the little devils one by one. Try to confine the alcohol to the infested area. Plants are teetotalers. Remember that alcohol has no residual effect. You may have missed the tiny mealy bug eggs, so check the plant every week or ten days for a month after application; 2) Nicotine sulphate and white oil sprays work well for serious invasions; and 3) mineral and vegetable oils are just about as effective for heavy infestations.

Aphids, also called "plant lice," are small (about one-eighth inch) but visible to the naked eye. They are usually black, but can be yellow, green, or pink, and prefer to colonize under leaves and on stems. As they suck sap from the plant, they exude a sweet, tacky substance called honeydew. Outdoors the honeydew attracts ants, and it is this sudden ant invasion that is one's first clue that a plant has aphids. The ants provide a "taxi service" in exchange for the honeydew, carrying aphids from one plant to another. Indoors you may not get the ant visitation to warn you. This is why periodic examination of your collection is imperative. Look for leaf curl and sooty black fungus which grows on the honeydew secretions.

Treatment: 1) Ladybug beetles seem to prefer aphids to any other food. You can try catching a few and placing them on the afflicted plant, or you may be able to purchase a small quantity from the organic gardening section of your nursery. For greater quantities, see the note at the end of this

Plant Parasites Chart

Aphids

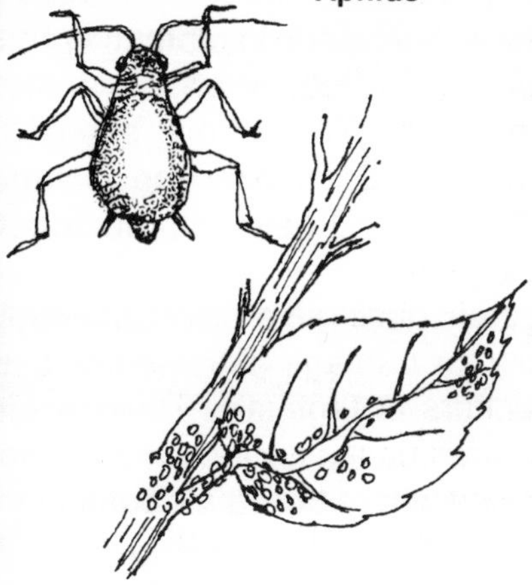

Spider Mites

Scale

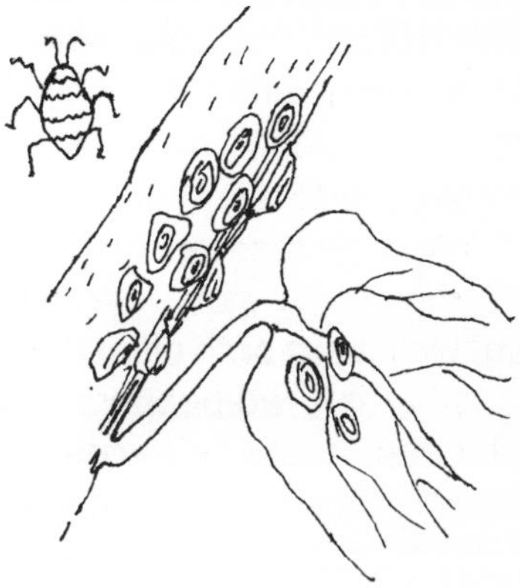

Mealybugs

Whiteflies

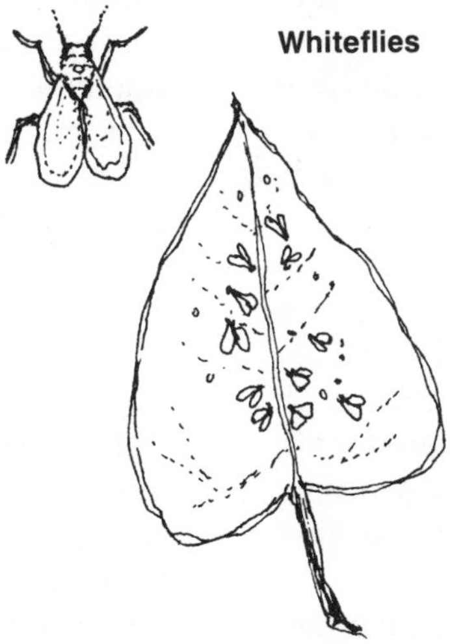

Thrips

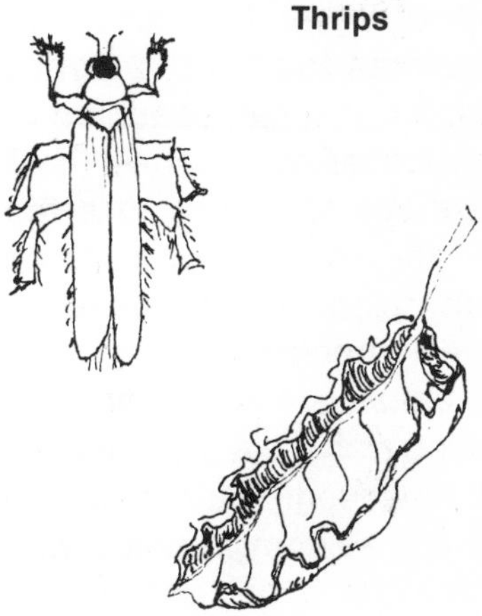

Earwigs

Slugs

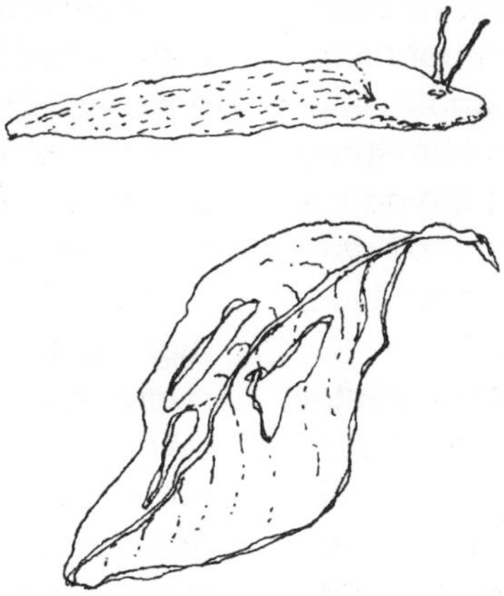

Grubs

chapter; 2) Some aphids are soil-borne and some attack roots. These can be dealt with safely either by pouring the contents of a bag of "Bull Durham" tobacco on the top soil and watering, or by soaking the bag in one cup of boiling water until the water takes on the color of strong tea, letting it cool to room temperature (tepid), then pouring the solution into the pot. The tobacco not only has an insecticide effect, it provides a little organic nourishment, as well; 3) A stronger treatment along the same lines is to spray the plant or dip its foliage in nicotine sulphate; 4) Use either rotenone (ROE'·ten·own) or pyrethrum (py·REETH'·rum), which are both plant derivatives; 5) Chop or grind either hot red peppers or green shallots in a food blender, add a little water, blend well and pour the liquid off into a hand mister (a perfume bottle with atomizer cap will work) and spray the plant thoroughly.

Red spider mites, like aphids, come in your choice of colors. They are almost impossible to detect without the aid of a strong (10x) magnifying glass, but you can see them by tapping some infested leaves over a sheet of white paper. The tiny critters scampering across the paper are mites. They are usually responsible when an otherwise healthy plant starts dropping leaves, or leaves suddenly become mottled or grayish. Often they try to emulate their distant cousins, the spiders, by spinning webs, but their spinning efforts are feeble by comparison. Plants that are misted or syringed daily are seldom troubled with mites since they loathe moist, humid conditions.

Treatment: 1) Try washing or spraying the entire foliage and stem with warm soap and water solutions first. This is often all that is needed; 2) A wheat flour-buttermilk spray is an effective treatment. Mix until you get a solution of the proper consistency to spray. Wet both the top and undersides of foliage and the stem; 3) Lime-sulphur spray works well; and 4) potassium sulphide (one ounce diluted in two gallons of water) can be used as a spray; or 5) nicotine sulphate can be used either as a spray or dip.

Scales are tough to eradicate, especially after they've established a beach head. The adult is protected from almost any assault under a hard, dull, waxy brown shell (scale) that, unfortunately, often goes unnoticed since it blends so well with the stem in tone and color. Once a year, usually in

spring, the adult female gives birth to a brood of young, who then crawl out from under their mother's shell to find their own juicy spot on which to feed.

Treatment: 1) First, either scrape the shell off with a thumbnail or with a toothbrush and soapy water. Then spray with a nicotine sulphate solution to kill any offspring; 2) Both rotenone and pyrethrum are effective. (NOTE: Our only success in coping with scale has been with the systemic poison, "Isotox." All other treatments have been only temporarily effective.)

Thrips. For their diminutive size (one-eighth inch), the capacity for damage of these tiny black or brown sap-suckers is fantastic. Their rasping mouth is used to open up a juicy vein in the tender new leaves of a plant where they suck contentedly away until discovered and dealt with or until the plant dies. Evidence of their presence is first seen as streaks of silvery residue and then in foliage that is curled and spotted brown and black. Thrips are particularly fond of *Ficus retusa nitida.* Almost never will thrips appear after the first three months a plant has been indoors. They are usually brought home with the plant from the nursery or hitch a ride inside on plants that have been outside for the summer.

Treatment: Use the same treatments as for red spider mite.

White fly is often brought inside at Christmas hiding under the leaves of the poinsettia. They are tiny, moth-like insects which stipple and devitalize foliage and leave a sticky sweet residue which causes sooty mold deposits on foliage and stem. When "host" plants are touched, white flies rise in a cloud, then settle again on their victim.

Treatment: 1) A strong spray of warm, soapy water may be effective, but probably only temporarily; 2) The plant extracts recommended previously—rotenone and pyrethrum—work well; 3) For ferns only, use nicotine sulphate, half a teaspoon diluted in a quart of warm, soapy water.

Most of the problems which afflict plants, other than invasions by predatory insects, are either directly caused, or aggravated by, their caretakers—us. Many plants are victims of our affinity for overly warm interiors. They simply can't survive day after day of hot, dry air. Even cacti and succulents occasionally like to have the humidity raised around them if they are sitting in the blazing sum-

Plant Maladies Chart

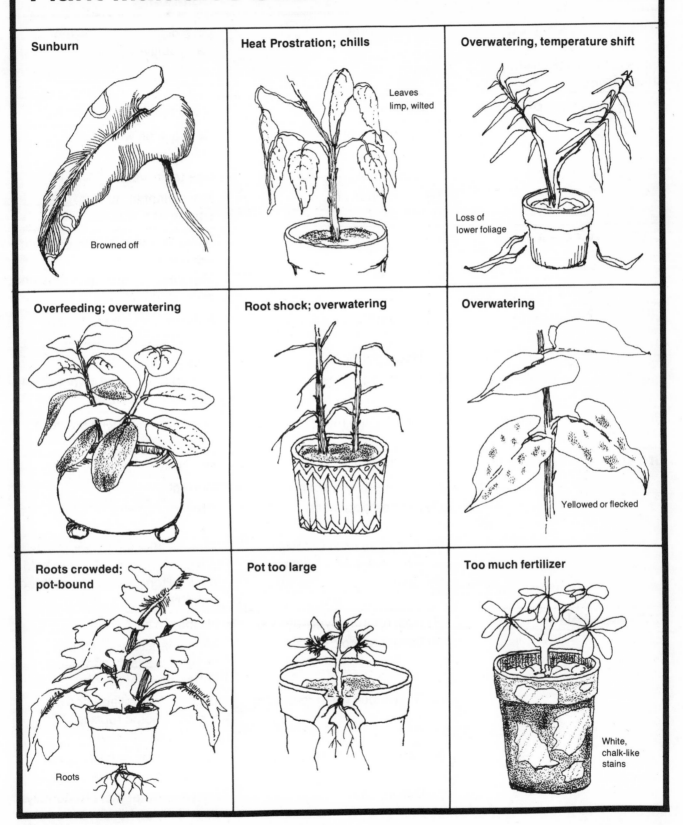

Sunburn

Browned off

Heat Prostration; chills

Leaves limp, wilted

Overwatering, temperature shift

Loss of lower foliage

Overfeeding; overwatering

Root shock; overwatering

Overwatering

Yellowed or flecked

Roots crowded; pot-bound

Roots

Pot too large

Too much fertilizer

White, chalk-like stains

ANALYZER CHART OF "HUMAN-CAUSED" PLANT PROBLEMS

Problem	Cause	Solution
Foliage yellowing, except for leaf veins. This is technically called chlorosis (loss of chlorophyll)	Insufficient iron in soil	Give plant a "booster shot" of iron additive
Paling (Etiolation) **of foliage**	Insufficient light	Move plant into brighter light
Leaf drop	(1) Over-watering	Cut back on water
	(2) Cold drafts	Move plant
	(3) Cold water	Use tepid water
	(4) Gas sensitivity	Move plant as far from gas source as possible
Dry, shriveled leaves	(1) Heat too high	Move to cooler spot or lower thermostat
	(2) Humidity too low	Mist daily or use pebble tray and water under plant
Little or weak growth	(1) Too little light	Either move plant to brighter area or supplement light
	(2) Roots pot-bound	Re-pot
	(3) Plant under-nourished	Feed plant (except in winter) with a complete fertilizer
Brown spots on leaves	Sunscorch; too much direct sun	Filter direct sun with shade or curtain
Brown tips or leaf edges	(1) Low humidity	Mist daily
	(2) Soil overly wet or dry	Correct
	(3) Poor air circulation	Change air inside at least once a day
	(4) Salt injury from excessive fertilizer, especially if high in nitrogen	Trim off affected foliage; flush out salts with lots of water; hold back all fertilizer for two or three months
Collapse of plant	(1) Root rot from overwatering	No known cure
	(2) Excessive cold or heat	Move plant to a spot which maintains a fairly consistent temperature of 68-70°
	(3) Root shock when re-potting	Cutting back foliage and trimming some roots is sometimes effective
	(4) Excessive fertilizer in soil	Try re-potting or flushing out excess mineral salts
	(5) Dehydration	Mist and water more frequently, especially on hot days

mer sun. Others fall prey to our enchantment with the watering can. Some of us seem determined to prepare our plants for the next Great Flood or the next Olympic swim.

Fungus diseases. **Leaf spot,** or **leaf blight,** is probably the most common of the fungi diseases which affect houseplants. It usually is the result of a combination of overly moist soil and stagnant air. The symptoms are white or pale patches on leaves and soft brown spots on stems. There may be black areas in the spots, which are the fruiting bodies of the fungus.

Control: Trim off and discard affected foliage. Treat the foliage and stem with a sulphur dust available at your local plant outlet. Give plants better ventilation, even on cold days.

Powdery mildew is a less common but troublesome fungus disease also brought on by high humidity and stagnant air. The symptoms are gray-white powder on patches of leaves and stem. Sometimes, the areas affected shrivel and dry out.

Control: Dusting with sulphur usually clears up the condition. Better air circulation prevents its recurrence.

Crown rot rarely plagues indoor gardeners, but it can occur if the conditions (high humidity and stagnant air) exist. The fungus, *Scleratium delphinii*, causes the plant crown to rot and topple.

Control: Plants which are afflicted with crown rot should be discarded. More efficient air circulation prevents its occurrence.

Root rot can be caused by several similar fungus organisms and is almost always the result of overwatering. The feeder roots decay and the plant starves to death.

Control: Plants affected should be discarded, along with the soil. Pots should be sterilized before being used again with boiling water at least five minutes for terra cotta pots, and an appropriate fungicide for plastic containers. In future, adopt stingy watering habits.

Springtails and **fungus gnats** are two common annoyances that often appear in the spring and summer when your plants are watered oftener and in greater volume. Their arrival is always precipitated by continually damp soil. While there is no evidence that they are harmful to established plants, though springtails can damage seedlings, the gnats can be a real nuisance. They're too small

to swat and just big enough to be bothersome, having a strong affinity for one's eyes. Fortunately, both can be controlled by allowing the soil to dry out between irrigations.

SPECIAL NOTE: Those who wish to use beneficial insects to control garden pests, indoors and out, may order them, at this writing, from the following sources.

Ladybugs, each of which consumes up to 50 aphids a day, are available at $6.50 a gallon (about 120,000 ladybugs per gallon) from: Bio-Control Company, Route 2, Box 2397, Auburn, CA 95603; L. E. Schnoor, Rough and Ready, CA 95975.

Praying Mantises, which feed on a multitude of predators, are available at $3 for eight (which will produce up to 400 voracious offspring) from: Eastern Biological Control Co., Route 5, Box 379, Jackson, New Jersey 08527; Gothard, Inc., P. O. Box 332, Canutillo, Texas 79835.

If these quantities are too large for your needs, share with other organic gardeners in your area or introduce your plant-loving friends to nature's way of pest control.

Myths, Fallacies, Old Wives' Tales & Hogwash

You need a green thumb to grow plants. Bosh! If you care enough about plants that you'll take the time to learn to care for them properly, you'll have enviable, show-quality results. It's the lazy gardener's cop out to say, "I tried to grow plants, but I don't have a green thumb." Many rank amateurs who didn't know their potash from a mole in the ground have grown specimens "impossible" to grow indoors because they cared and were observant.

Manure is the best fertilizer for all plants. Horse-feathers! Manure is a very weak fertilizer (depending upon the animal's diet), but it's good as a soil amendment for outdoor gardens. Some plants are supposed to do better when well-rotted manure is added to the soil, but we've found even these can survive without it.

Indoor gardening is for women. Pshaw! This is a holdover of male chauvinism. Although the attitude is changing, there is still a prevalent belief among the majority of macho-oriented males that there is something not quite, well—*normal*—about a guy who fools around with plants and flowers indoors. What difference does it really make *where* one does one's gardening? Gardening, indoors, or out, is an asexual vocation or hobby. The only important thing is to do it. In a world fast becoming paved over, polluted, strip mined, dammed, and denuded of forests, we need all the help we can get. One gardener (particularly an organic gardener) does more to restore the ecological balance of our planet than all the rhetoric from a hundred self-styled ecologists.

Plants like to drink from a saucer. Nosireebob! Countless hundreds of plants have been drowned by this little gem of misinformation. As indicated elsewhere in this book, plants do benefit from sitting in a saucer or tray of pebbles which are covered with water. But when the water level reaches the base of the pot, so that the moisture is entering the drainage hole—and when this condition persists for days—root rot and soured soil are the inevitable consequences.

Plants need a little sunbath to revitalize them. Nix! It is a frustrating experience to see family and friends putting plants we've given them outside in direct sunlight, even after they've been advised that this is potentially fatal to acclimated plants. Some people just will not accept the fact that direct sun can severely burn tender, sensitive foliage in a matter of minutes. They see outdoor plants, flowers, and trees thriving in the sun, so they decide a little sunbath couldn't hurt their plants. When the plants totally collapse, these people attribute their demise to a multitude of sinister or supernatural influences, such as the position of Uranus in relation to the North Star, or the effects of gamma rays from the Polaris submarine. Just as your skin is sensitive to sun after a long winter, the foliage of a plant that has lived indoors all year is likewise tender.

Plants rob the air of oxygen. Poppycock! Plants *do* remove some oxygen from the air, but they produce far more oxygen than they take. Plants actually *improve* the quality of the air you breathe.

Drafts are harmful to plants. Only partially true. Cold, wintry blasts are definitely debilitating, but a warm, summery breeze that gently caresses the foliage is therapeutic.

Air conditioners are detrimental to plants. Another partial truth. As long as plants are six feet or further from the vents, no harm is done, in our experience. Instead, most plants thrive in air-conditioned environments, even though the dehumidifiers on most systems remove the moisture content of the air. You can replace the moisture by using vaporizers, humidifiers, or simple hand misters and atomizers.

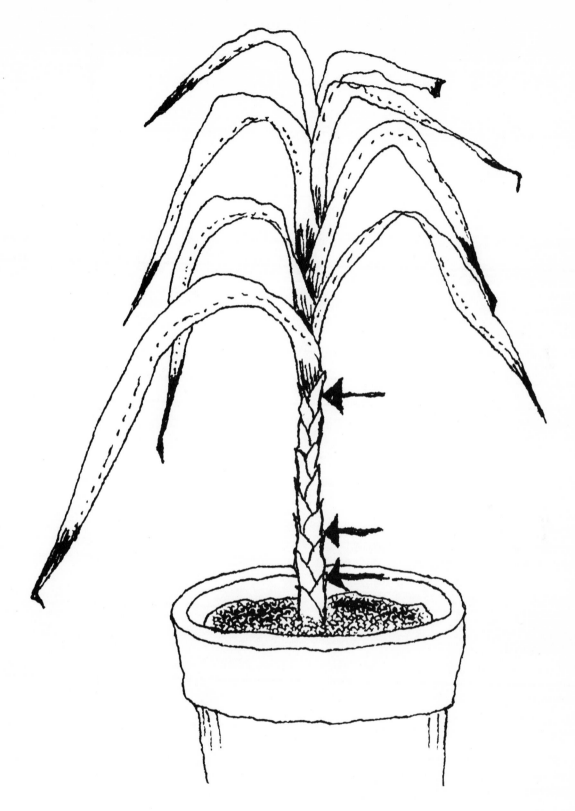

Sick or damaged plants, such as this Dracaena, can be salvaged by cutting back at any of the three places indicated.

Chapter 8

50 Plants & How to Grow Them

Acalypha wilkesiana macafeana

Common name: Copperleaf; beefsteak plant
Nativity: New Hebrides, Ceylon

This colorful, bushy shrub is often chosen as a substitute for flowers, since its bright hues don't fade, providing an emotional lift on dreary winter days. The copperleaf's large (up to nine inches) leaves are mottled with bronze and pinkish red and these colors are accented even more strongly with high-intensity natural light. It also gives a bonus of red blooms seasonally. With good light (some sun) and ideal care, copperleafs can grow to five and even six feet indoors, but three feet is average. Taller plants tend to "go leggy" and pruning helps keep the foliage thick and compactly set on the branches. Old, deteriorating plants may be cut

back in spring and will recover nicely within the year. For a more unusual variety, try *Acalypha hispida*, commonly called "chenille plant," or "red hot cat tail." This East Indian native has bold green or copper-colored foliage and flowers which hang down as bright red tassels reminiscent of chenille. Once it blooms, it retains the flowers year round, if given some sun and good horticultural care. Although *A. hispida* is seldom seen as anything but a windowsill specimen, it is available as a mature plant at many nurseries and can grow to eight or nine feet with proper care. Selective pruning will prevent it from outgrowing its allotted space. As the plant matures, the tassels can extend to nearly two feet.

Use *Acalypha* in any window situation where color is desired, but protect from intense summer sun.

Basic care. Acclimation: None required. **Soil:** Thrives in a rich, fibrous basic soil a bit on the acid side (add an extra trowel of shredded peat moss or leaf mold). Keep evenly moist spring through fall and on the dry side through the winter. **Light:** The plant needs about four hours of winter sun or bright light and can take filtered sun in summer; but it probably will do well if you can provide continuous direct light or diffuse, bright light. Sun helps intensify colors in the foliage and encourage blooms. **Temperature:** A warmth-lover, *Acalpha* does best in a range of 60° at night to 80° during the day. **Humidity:** Keep humidity high. **Fertilizer:** Feed with a complete fertilizer every month from spring to fall, beginning four to six months after purchase. **Propagation:** Propagate from stem cuttings.

Acalypha wilkesiana macafeana

Acanthus mollis

Common name: Bears breech
Nativity: Southern Europe

A durable, easy-care perennial is the bears breech which has no stem or trunk, in the traditional sense, but produces its attractive, lobed, dark-green leaves from a fleshy rhizome (RYE′zoam), which is an underground rootlike stem. At maturity, its leaves are about two or three feet long and, if given some sun, the plant will bloom in spring with white or purplish spikes of tubular flowers. If you're after more impressive foliage, the flower stalks should be removed before they bloom. Three family members which are not as easy or striking are: *A. m.* '*Latifolius,*' which grows larger by about a foot; *A. montanus*, or "mountain thistle," an African native, which has spine-studded leaves up to a foot long and usually grows to maturity (four feet tall) the first year; and *A. spinosus*, which is similar to *A. montanus* and produces purple flowers and dense spikes. The leaves of this variety greatly influenced early art and appear in stylized form on many Greek Corinthian columns.

Use *Acanthus* in any partially-sunny situation. Its durability and unfussiness help it adapt easily in places many other plants would fail.

Basic care. Acclimation: None required. Even established plants in five-gallon cans go directly indoors without difficulty. **Soil:** A basic mix with extra sand for rapid drainage kept evenly moist. In hot weather, the plant may require more water than most plants. **Light:** Some sun in summer and maximum winter sun produces the hardiest specimens and is vital if you want the plant to bloom. Otherwise, bright, diffuse light year round is fine. You may get by with only medium bright light, but the plant does not respond well in dark spots. **Temperature:** The normal household ranges are acceptable to *A. mollis*. Recommended ideal levels are . . . nighttime, around 50° to 55°, daytime about 70°. **Humidity:** Average year round, with good ventilation in hot weather. *A. mollis* likes to have its leaves washed once a week and responds to misting once a day from spring through the summer. **Fertilizer:** Feed monthly from spring to fall with a complete fertilizer diluted at half strength. **Propagation:** Propagate from seeds, or by division of the rhizome in spring or fall.

Acanthus mollis

Aloe

Nativity: Primarily South Africa

These unusual succulents offer a wide range of foliage structure and coloring; and nearly all of them produce beautiful blooms monthly or annually, although they must be given optimum care to encourage blooming indoors. They range in height from four inches to tree-type giants of eighteen feet. If they are summered outdoors and wintered indoors, they achieve greater height and are more inclined to produce flowers, but they can be grown successfully indoors all year.

A. arborescens, or candelabra aloe, has thick, spiny-edged, bluish-green leaves; height average is twelve feet, although if it is grown in an ideal outdoor location it can become much taller. Blooms are red and yellow in late winter.

A. ciliaris has thick stems which grow to eight feet, sometimes ten feet. Leaves are thick and deep green. Blooms appear on stalks in clusters, usually in late winter, and are green or yellow.

A. ferox may become too large for an indoor situation. Its thick, stout, trunky stem soars to fourteen feet and is adorned with rosettes of spiny green leaves one foot to two feet long. Deep, vibrant red flower clusters appear seasonally.

A. nobilis, or gold-spined aloe, may reach a height of two feet and is characterized by shark-like teeth on the perimeter of its grayish-green leaves. Flowers of crimson and gold rise on stalks one and a half to two feet tall in midsummer.

Use all the aloes in sunny window locations, or to create an interesting succulent garden if you have unlimited space.

Basic care. Acclimation: None is needed. All go from the nursery to a sun-drenched interior location without difficulty. **Soil:** All do best in a basic soil mix laced with extra sand for fast drainage, with the amendment of one tablespoon of limestone to each gallon of planting medium. Also add two tablespoons of steamed bonemeal to the bottom layer of soil in each pot. Keep soil on the dry side; let it dry to a depth of two inches before irrigating again. **Light:** Aloes need some summer sun; maximum winter sun; and bright, diffuse light all year. Sun encourages blooms, but is not vital to successful cultivation of aloes indoors. **Temperature:** On the warm side: 50° to 55° at night, 65° to 75° by day. The plants will accept higher or lower ranges without difficulty. **Humidity:** Average. Occasionally wipe foliage to remove dust and enhance appearance. **Fertilizer:** Newly acquired plants should not be fed the first year. The second year, feed with a complete fertilizer in late summer only. **Propagation:** Most aloes produce suckers or offsets, which can be removed and rooted in moist sand to increase your stock. Set suckers aside for three days so that cut ends can callus before placing them in sand to root.

Aloe

Alsophila cooperi *(A. australis)*

Common name: Australian tree fern
Nativity: Tasmania

The Australian tree fern is often mistakenly called by the name of its close relative, *Dicksonia antarctica* (Tasmanian tree fern). It matters very little, since both require the same care. Tree ferns, like most other ferns, are very difficult to grow indoors, except in greenhouses where the cool, moist air they require is provided for them consistently. If you're willing to pamper them almost daily during the summer, and can give them a cool, moist, brightly illuminated location with no sun, you may succeed where most others fail. Characteristics of *A. cooperi* are a brown, hairy trunk from the tip of which grows emerald-green, delicately structured, arching fronds which at maturity reach eleven feet in length. A mature fern growing outdoors may attain heights of fifteen to twenty feet.

Use *A. cooperi* as the focal point for such areas as a skylit indoor fountain, a glassed-in sunporch with east or south exposure, or near a brightly illuminated window. It will dominate an entire corner if growing conditions are adequate. A plant that has outgrown the space you can alot to it can go on a sheltered patio, balcony, or a side of the house that gets only morning summer sun. It is hardy to 30°.

Basic care. Acclimation: Keep the humidity high the first two weeks after you bring it inside. It can go from the lath house directly indoors. Keep its soil moist, and water the top and trunk when you irrigate the soil. Mist the fronds twice a day, but do so early enough in the day so that the moisture will evaporate before nightfall. **Soil:** A special mix of fir bark and sand with a little leaf mold produces the best results. Keep the mix evenly moist, particularly in the late spring and through the summer. **Light:** It thrives in full winter sun; but bright, diffuse light will suffice all year.

Temperature: A night range of 50° to 60° and a day range of 65° to 70° is ideal, although with patience you can adapt the plant to cooler or warmer levels. **Humidity:** High humidity is the order of the day. During hot summer days, you may have to mist or syringe six or seven times. Ideally the container holding the plant should be set on a pebble-filled tray with water not quite up to the base of the pot. The rising waves of moist air from the tray keep the foliage tips fresh and green. This will also cut down on the need for frequent hand misting.

Covering the top soil with polished rocks or sphagnum moss helps retain soil moisture. With the advent of winter, you can cut back on the amount of water you put in the container; but continue to mist and irrigate the trunk, since the heating system will rob the air of most of its moisture. If humidity is too low, the growing tips and ends of the fronds will begin to wilt and become dry and brittle. **Fertilizer:** Feed monthly 'til fall with organic fertilizer.

Alsophila cooperi (Australian tree fern)

Ananas comosus *(Pineapple)*

Common name: Hawaiian pineapple
Nativity: South America

Of all the bromeliads, the pineapple is probably the most unusual and fascinating, particularly if you can induce it to fruit indoors. This is no mean task as it involves about a two-year wait, and often your indulgence and patience are not rewarded. As frequently as an indoor-grown *A. comosus* produces fruit, it just as frequently doesn't, so you may want to consider buying a specimen already fruited. *A. comosus* grows to thirty-six inches and produces dark green leaves. Even without fruit, it makes an interesting addition to a plant collection.

If you want to try growing your own, separate the crown (the green top) from the fruit of a pineapple leaving about an inch of the "meat" attached. Put the crown aside and let it dry for a couple of days, then pot it up in a five-inch terra cotta container (or what-have-you) with a mixture of sand, peat moss, and sphagnum moss, or with fir bark and sand. Bring the soil level up to the base of the crown. Water well and add a little liquid fertilizer containing chelated iron into the top of the crown. A dilution of quarter-strength is recommended to prevent burning

Ananas comosus (Pineapple)

the foliage. Pineapples are primarily epiphytic, like some orchids, which means they are capable of absorbing and utilizing moisture and nutrients from the air. For this reason they are rather shallow-rooted, since they don't have to rely on a complex feeder-root system for nourishment and survival. Set the potted crown in a window that gets bright natural light. Some sun encourages fruiting, but a west window exposure may be too hot. The fruit develops in summer from bracts which appear on spikes. These are fused together by the plant and evolve into the pineapple.

Basic care. Acclimation: Plants obtained from the nursery need little or no acclimation. They can go directly to a warm, bright window location. **Soil:** A soil composed primarily of fir bark laced with sand is recommended; a rich, organic, acid soil is a good alternative planting medium. Keep the soil on the dry side by saturating it, then allowing it to dry out to a depth of two inches before irrigating again. **Light:** Pineapples like some sun but need at least very bright illumination to thrive. Plants won't fruit in dim light. **Temperature:** The plants prefer a *consistently* warm environment above 65° day and night. If the temperature dips below 65°, the plant may go dormant. It can take 80° on a regular basis only with adequate moisture. **Humidity:** Average. Occasional misting into the crown is beneficial. **Fertilizer:** Use liquid fertilizer high in acid content diluted at quarter-strength and feed every third of fourth week in the soil and in the crown. Twice a year, give the plant a "shot" of liquid iron to perk it up. **Propagation:** Propagate from offsets at the side or top of the plant after these have produced four to six leaves. Rooting can best be accomplished in a medium of half sand and half milled peat moss. Or propagate by rooting tops.

Araucaria heterophylla

Common names: Norfolk Island pine; star pine
Nativity: Norfolk Island (South Pacific)

This beautiful native of a tiny island in the South Seas makes an ideal living Christmas tree which doesn't have to go outdoors after the holidays. As a seedling tree it grows in almost symmetrical perfection, with overlapping branches covered with hundreds of pine-needle-like leaves a quarter-inch long. As the tree matures, the leaves lengthen to over an inch and the branches are more widely spaced, exposing more of the trunk; they tend to droop under the weight of the foliage. In its native habitat, very old trees reach two hundred feet in height. Indoors, five to six feet is average. *A. heterophylla* is a slow-grower by most standards, adding only four to six inches a year. This is part of the reason greenhouse-grown specimens are so costly (up to $125). Field-grown specimens, which adapt well indoors, can be acquired very reasonably when one considers the size being offered—a four-footer in a five-gallon can sometimes can be found for about nine dollars. Never prune *A. heterophylla*. If growing tips are cut, they will not be replaced, as with most plants; and never cut back the top. This would ruin the shape of the tree permanently.

Use the Norfolk pine in any cool location that gets bright, diffuse light. Can take some winter sun. Field-grown specimens not under lath may have adjusted to more sun than the tree normally can endure. In this case, try a sunny location first; it may like it there.

Basic care. Acclimation: Most specimens can be treated as houseplants without preliminaries. Simply keep the plant cool and in a high-humidity situation for the first two weeks. **Soil:** It needs an acid soil kept evenly moist through the summer and kept on the dry side in winter. **Light:** Bright, diffuse light is best with some winter sun. Field-grown specimens not under lath may be able to handle unfiltered sun from an eastern exposure. **Temperature:** It favors the cool range of 50° to 55° by day, but adapts easily to both higher and lower variations. **Humidity:** Average. Mist to freshen foliage once a day in summer and a couple of times a week in winter. **Fertilizer:** After four to six months, feed monthly from spring to fall with an acid fertilizer. **Propagation:** Start all over with new plants.

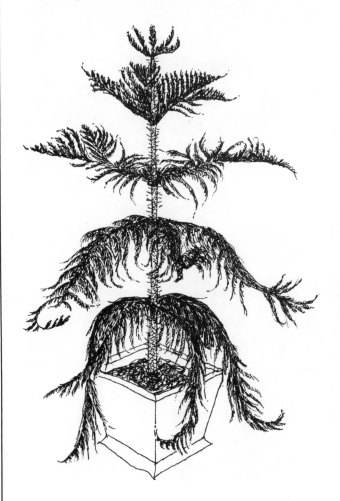

Araucaria heterophylla

Asparagus

Nativity: Primarily South Africa

There are over one hundred varieties of asparagus, and of these, four adapt well to indoor cultivation: *A. plumosus*, *A. meyerii*, *A. retrofractus*, and *A. sprengerii*. All four have the foliage characteristics of the species —minute, needle-like "leaves," which are not technically leaves but are flat branches called *cladodes*. They are ideal houseplants for those who like to water their collections more often than they require. Most can take irrigation every other day, provided they're potted up in fast-draining soil.

A. plumosus, or emerald feather, is usually seen as a dwarf variety not exceeding three feet, but the standard variety grows to eighteen feet and averages fifteen. Its sprays of fern-like fronds are highly favored by florists to dress up floral arrangements. Seasonally it produces small white flowers and black berries.

A. meyerii, plume or foxtail asparagus, grows in upright fluffy plumes two to three feet tall.

A. retrofractus. Foliage appears from willowy, silver-gray branches up to eight feet long that at first resemble elongated asparagus. Its delicate-looking, one-inch "leaves" are carried at the tips of a well-developed branch system in deep green tufts. It has a tendency to grow upright, eventually achieving a tree-like appearance, but pinching back growing tips encourages bushiness. Outdoors, *A. retrofractus* produces small white flowers in clusters, though it seldom blooms indoors.

A. sprengerii, or Sprenger fern, like *A. retrofractus* and others, is not technically a fern, but a member of the lily family. Best known of the asparagus species, *A. sprengerii* produces spiny stems up to six feet long covered with compactly set half-inch "needles." It is one of the fastest growers in the plant kingdom, achieving three to four feet of growth and filling out well in just a couple of months. Keeping it crowded in a small pot encourages greater bulk. Outdoors it produces pink flowers and red berries, sometimes simultaneously.

Use asparagus ferns in well-lit bathrooms and kitchens, particularly *A. sprengerii* in hanging baskets. They all respond to high humidity and warmth, particularly in winter.

Basic care. Acclimation: None is needed. **Soil:** A basic, fast-draining soil mix kept evenly moist works well for all. During the summer, all require much more water than most other plants. *A. sprengerii*, especially, may need irrigation every other day to thrive. The soil must not become boggy, so make certain excess water drains through and is dumped from the saucer. Some water over pebbles in the saucer or underliner is beneficial. **Light:** Most field-grown specimens can take some direct summer sun. Greenhouse-grown plants may suffer from direct sun. Both can take full winter sun and require bright, diffuse light the year around. Dim light prompts leaves to pale or yellow off. **Temperature:** They are not too particular about temperature; the normal interior range suffices. Ideal levels are 55° to 60° at night, 65° to 75° by day. **Humidity:** High humidity in summer, average in winter. Mist once or twice a day during hot weather. **Fertilizer:** Feed with a complete fertilizer from spring through fall each month. High water requirements may cause some chlorosis. If leaves begin to yellow, even though plant is in good light, apply chelated iron to correct. **Propagation:** By division of clumps, or from berries planted half an inch deep.

Asparagus

Asplenium

Nativity: New Zealand and Malaya

Those who have "a way" with ferns may want to try one or all three of the commonly available Asplenium, or spleenwort, species—*A. bulbiferum* (mother fern); *A. nidus* (bird's nest); or *A. viviparum* (Mauritius mother fern). Both *A. bulbiferum* and *A. viviparum* produce minute plantlets on the tops of mature fronds in spring and summer which can be re-

moved and rooted. *A. nidus* has glossy undivided fronds which grow from a core of black, fibrous strands which call to mind a bird's nest,

Asplenium bulbiferum

hence the common name. Both *A. bulbiferum* and *A. viviparum* require the high humidity and soil moisture which call for daily attention and make them unsuitable for the indifferent gardener. Although *A. nidus* is more tolerant of neglect, it also needs more care than other typical plants. In short, if you can't devote a few minutes daily to caring for these (and other) ferns, try other less demanding species.

Probably the best location for *Aspleniums* is a bathroom which gets good light.

Basic care. Acclimation: None required. **Soil:** The packaged mix marketed as "African Violet soil," works well with these ferns. Otherwise, use a basic mix with sand and horticultural charcoal (one cup each per gallon of mix). Both mother ferns may need daily soaking in hot weather while the bird's nest may require heavy watering only every third day. Keep the soil barely moist through the winter. **Light:** All three do best in bright, diffuse light, generally speaking, but some fern fanciers succeed with only medium light. No sun anytime for these. **Temperature:** The normal interior ranges suffice. **Humidity:** High humidity is part of the secret of growing ferns. A tray of water-covered pebbles may eliminate the frequent misting which would otherwise be necessary from late spring through the summer. **Fertilizer:** Plant food is not essential. Feed only once a year, in late spring with a complete fertilizer at half strength. **Propagation:** Use the tiny bulbs, or plantlets, on mother ferns to increase your stock.

Aucuba japonica

Common name: Japanese aucuba
Nativity: Japan and Asia

There are several cultivars of Aucuba, all of which grow well indoors in cool locations; they do even better wintering indoors and summering in a shady nook on patios and balconies. The standard *A. japonica* grows to about five feet indoors but takes off outdoors to reach fourteen or more feet eventually. It's a shrubby spreader and is characterized by deep green, serrated leaves two to three inches wide, and depending upon maturity, two to eight inches

long. It responds well to pruning at the leaf joints before spring or in early spring. Although *A. japonica* blooms, producing small, reddish-

purple flower clusters and red berries, it may not bloom indoors. Other popular varieties of Aucuba are *A. j. longifolia*, which produces long, willowy leaves; *A. j. nana*, a dwarf which achieves a height of only two or three feet; and *A. j. variegata*, which is probably the most universally collected and cultivated variety, also commonly called "gold dust plant." Its deep green foliage looks as though it was splashed with a bucket of yellow paint.

Use *A. japonicas* on unheated sunporches or any other spot where the temperature remains below 65°. Because of their preference for bright illumination and coolness, their use indoors is rather limited.

Basic care. Acclimation: None is required if you can provide a bright, cool situation. **Soil:** An acid soil or a basic mix slightly on the acid side should be kept barely moist. Water when the soil is dry to a depth of one inch. Excessive moisture is fatal to *A. japonica*. **Light:** A shade-lover outdoors, it needs bright, diffuse light indoors and may tolerate winter sun, but no direct summer sun. **Temperature:** Coolness is essential to the well-being of this plant. A night temperature around 50° and a day level not higher than 65° is ideal. It may adapt to slightly warmer temperatures with time. **Humidity:** High humidity in summer, average in winter. Mist daily during hot weather and create a cooling microclimate with water-covered pebbles in a tray or saucer under the plant. **Fertilizer:** Feed every two months with an acid fertilizer from spring to fall. **Propagation:** From stem or root cuttings.

Aucuba japonica 'Variegata' (Gold Dust plant)

Bamboo

Nativity: Asia

Of the many varieties of bamboo, there are four which adapt well to indoor cultivation, particularly if they winter indoors and summer outdoors. All require bright light and good ventilation to thrive. It should be noted that most are "messy" indoor plants in that they frequently drop dead foliage. This isn't a problem outdoors but inside it means that you'll be continually tidying up after the plant. Dead canes that are pruned off must be removed to the root line. Stumps that are left eventually decay and can kill the entire plant.

Bambusa multiplex, or Chinese Goddess, is native to Asia in general and Vietnam in particular. It produces a mix of gold and green fern-like leaves and reedy, hollow stems which reach six feet in height.

B. nana is a dwarf by comparison with most varieties, reaching only three and a half to four feet with three-inch bluish-green leaves.

B. phyllostachys aurea, or golden bamboo, grows to ten feet under ideal conditions and requires more water than other varieties.

B. nigra, black bamboo, is probably the most striking of all with its ebony stems which average six feet in height but can grow to eight and nine feet with optimum care. It needs very bright light.

Use bamboo as a privacy screen instead of drapes in a window which gets intense natural light but little, if any, sun.

Basic care. Acclimation: Field-grown bamboo should be given a two-week period in a cool, shady spot before re-potting and moving inside. Select a location indoors that gets bright, diffuse light and good ventilation. Keep the plant well watered. **Soil:** A basic soil mix should be kept evenly moist after acclimation. **Light:** All bamboo varieties need bright, diffuse light to thrive. **Temperature:** A cool range of 50° to 55° at night and 60° to 65° by day is recommended, but most plants can adapt to levels a bit cooler or warmer. **Humidity:** Average humidity suffices. **Fertilizer:** Feed monthly with a complete fertilizer from spring to fall. **Propagation:** By division of root clumps or by layering young shoots.

NOTE: Bamboo can go for years in the original container. This encourages fuller growth. But division and potting on every three years is the normal cultivation practice and is a way of increasing your stock. Also, bamboo that seems reluctant to adapt indoors should come back strong if you return it outdoors for the summer and bring it back inside in winter. You might try alternating two plants, so you have one indoors continuously. If you do move the plant outside, keep it in shade so you won't have to repeat the acclimation process when winter comes.

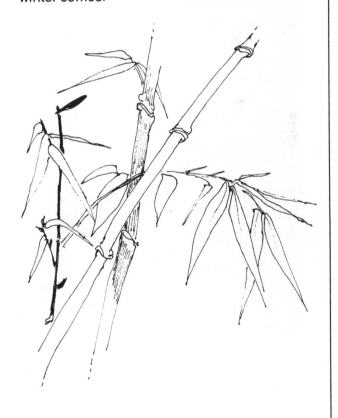

Bamboo

Banana

Nativity: Africa and other temperate locales

You shouldn't really expect a banana harvest, no matter how gifted an indoor gardener you are, but banana trees make bold-leafed, fast-growing, showy plants, particularly if you start with an established tree rather than from seeds. There are standard plants, which grow from twelve to fifteen feet high, and dwarfs which seldom exceed a height of two feet. If you decide to try a banana tree indoors, try to find one of the dwarfs at your local nursery. They're easier to handle and don't outgrow their allotted space.

Musa cavendishii, or *M. nana*, grows to about five feet indoors and produces blue-green, red-splotched leaves eight to ten inches wide and one and a half feet to two feet long.

M. ensete maurelii, or Ethiopian banana, grows to about fourteen feet outdoors and may reach any height up to that limit indoors. It has large, red-edged leaves and leaf stalks.

M. mannii is a two-foot dwarf with a thin stem accented with black and four-inch to six-inch-wide leaves which grow to about two feet in length.

Use banana trees in any brightly illuminated location. Allocate a lot of space (four by four feet for a five-year-old plant), since most spread out.

Basic care. Acclimation: No adaptation period is required. Keep the tree cool and the humidity high for the first two weeks. **Soil:** Banana trees thrive in acid soil kept evenly moist in summer and slightly dry in winter. **Light:** Bright, diffuse light is required the year around. The plant can take maximum winter sun and some summer sun, but watch for sunburn on the leaves. **Temperature:** Most plants adjust to normal household levels. Good ventilation becomes more important as temperature rises above 75°. **Humidity:** High humidity helps balance moisture loss from wide leaf surfaces when the plant is grown indoors. Mist frequently during hot weather, and in winter wipe foliage weekly with a damp cloth to refresh and remove dust. **Fertilizer:** Feed monthly from spring to fall with a complete acid fertilizer at full strength. **Propagation:** From cuttings or start with new plants from the nursery. You can also propagate from seeds, but with seed propagation impressive results are a long way off.

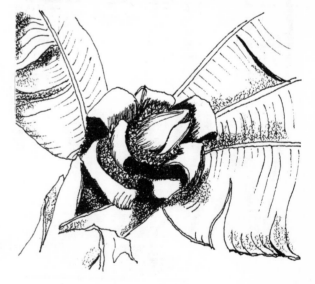

Banana

Beaucarnea recurvata

Common names: Bottle palm; elephant-foot tree; pony tail
Nativity: Mexican and Texas deserts

Scarce and costly in the larger sizes (over three feet), this unusual member of the yucca family has a clumpy, ridged, bulbous trunk (two or three trunks in very old specimens) which develops, as do we humans, deeper wrinkles as it ages. The trunk, which is composed of water-storing tissues which carry the plant safely through the frequent droughts of its native habitat, is widest at the soil line and gradually tapers inward. It is topped by a tuft of grassy leaves up to four feet long. The edges of the leaves are razor-sharp, so handle same with care. The succulent capacity of the plant makes re-potting easy since *B. recurvata* can live for days on its water reservoir if uprooted. It is an extremely slow grower, but eventually attains a height of twenty-five feet. Re-potting is seldom necessary for at least five years, but annual top dressing is recommended.

Use the plant in any warm, brightly illuminated spot. It is a natural for a sunny window in summer and winter. On very hot days a thin curtain may be necessary between the plant and the window to protect tender new foliage.

Basic care. Acclimation: This is one of the few plants which doesn't suffer from the sudden change from outdoors to indoors. It settles in nicely with a little sun and warmth. **Soil:** Although it's a denizen of the desert, it seems to do best in a basic soil mix, rather than a cactus mix, but you should add extra sand for good drainage, as well as one and a half to two tablespoons of limestone to a gallon of planting mix. Keep the mix on the dry side. Remember, *B. recurvata* is a succulent type and too much water is a threat to its well-being. **Light:** It likes some sun the year around, but will survive with only bright, diffuse light. **Temperature:** A warmth lover, it should have about 60° to 65° at night and 80° to 85° by day with good ventilation. It suffers above 100° and dies at 20°. **Humidity:** Average. Mist once a week. **Fertilizer:** Feed only twice a year, in early spring and late summer, with a complete fertilizer at full strength. **Propagation:** From seeds any time of the year.

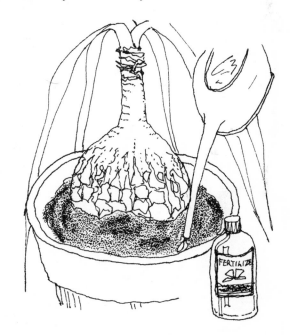

Beaucarnea recurvata

Bougainvillea

Common name: Paper flower
Nativity: South America, particularly Brazil

Bougainvillea is one of the few sun-loving plants which can come directly inside to a sunny location without an adjustment period, and—contrary to what is commonly believed—it thrives indoors. In an ideal indoor location, there seems to be no limit to its growth potential, but cutting back is usually required to keep it under control. Care should be taken when potting up from the nursery can, since bougainvillea does not form a typical root ball. Keep as much soil as you can around the roots and take pains to disturb them as little as pos-sible during the operation. In addition to attrac-tive, heart-shaped foliage, all varieties produce brilliantly-colored bracts surrounding tiny flow-ers to create a dazzling floral display, and most seem willing to put on this exhibition indoors, unlike some flowering species which are brought inside. Some of the more spectacular varieties are:

B. Barbara Karst. Tall, bushy, vigorous growth. An early bloomer which produces crimson bracts which may take on a blue tinge indoors.

B. Betty Hendry, or "Indian Maid," is often tri-colored in red, yellow and purple.

B. Scarlet O'Hara produces dark green leaves and long-lived crimson bracts.

B. Temple Fire is a shrubby spreader which may drop some foliage. Produces red bracts.

Use bougainvillea in a sunny situation. Can even take sun through a west window in sum-mer with good ventilation.

Basic care. Acclimation: None re-quired. **Soil:** A basic mix with a cup each of sand and charcoal to a gallon of potting medium. Keep evenly moist from spring to summer, then barely moist to encourage good floral production. **Light:** Sun, summer and winter, is required to induce indoor blooming, but will survive and, perhaps, even bloom in bright, diffuse light. Does not respond well in dim or dark locations. **Temperature:** Adjusts well in a range of 65° night to 75° day. Most are willing to settle for what you can give them. **Humidity:** Daily misting in hot weather is re-commended. **Fertilizer:** Feed in early spring and early summer with a complete fertilizer at full strength. **Propagation:** From cuttings.

Bougainvillea

Carissa grandiflora

Common name: Natal plum
Nativity: South Africa

If you have a sunny spot which will accommodate the natal plum, you should get—in addition to attractive, heart-shaped foliage——aromatic white flowers which are followed (with hand pollination) by plum-like red fruit, or berries, which are similar in taste to tart cranberries. The fruit is first green then ripens to a crimson red, and can be used to make sauces or jams, if enough are produced. The plant's

natural tendency is toward shrubbiness and, since it responds well to pruning and trimming, is often used in hedges. It is a fast-grower and may reach two or three feet the first year—a feat few other plants can duplicate. A variety more commonly tried indoors is *C. g. 'Boxwood Beauty'* which seldom grows taller or wider than two feet and doesn't have the spines that are characteristic of the species. The ovate leaves of this variety are compactly

set in pairs and overlap. Even more widely known and collected as a houseplant is *C. g. nana compacta* (may be sold as *C. g. 'Tuttle'*), which closely resembles 'Boxwood Beauty' and is often chosen as a bonsai candidate. Other varieties which can be found in most nurseries from coast to coast are *C. g. 'Fancy,'* which should reach five feet after a couple of years; *C. g. 'Minima,'* which may slowly grow to two feet; and *C. g. 'Tomlinson,'* a dwarf spreader which should achieve two feet of height and width and has unusual glossy, maroon foliage plus showy flowers.

Use *C. grandiflora* in any sunny location which is also cool at night.

Basic care. Acclimation: None required, even with larger (five-gallon) specimens. Move directly to a sunny spot and keep humidity high. **Soil:**   A basic mix with extra sand kept evenly moist until winter, then barely moist. **Light:**   Some summer sun is essential to successful cultivation and production of blossoms and fruit. Will survive in bright, diffuse light, but it is doubtful that flowers will appear without some sun for a few hours daily. **Temperature:**   Prefers a slightly cool environment—50°-55° at night and not much above 68° during the day. Will take warmer daytime temperatures with good ventilation but needs a sharp drop at night, at least the first year. **Humidity:**   High humidity during warm weather and vigorous growth period. A pebble-filled tray containing some water under the plant is very beneficial. Frequent misting stimulates bud production. Cut down on humidity in late fall and throughout the winter months. **Fertilizer:** Feed every two months from spring to fall with a complete fertilizer at full strength. **Propagation:** From cuttings.

Carissa grandiflora "Tuttle"

Chamaedorea *(Palms)*

Nativity: Central America and other temperate locales

This family of palms grows well indoors and is tolerant of low light and neglect; most members are slow growers, so they don't make additional space demands for a number of years.

C. cataractarum eventually grows to five feet from a stout trunk.

C. ernesti-augusti. Dark green, fishtail leaves. This one slowly grows to four feet or sometimes five feet.

C. glaucifolia produces feather-type fronds about five feet long, and after a few years, it grows to nine feet outdoors; four feet indoors is average.

C. seifrizii is probably the most foolproof as an indoor candidate. It is a cluster palm (clump forming), growing to ten feet outdoors and four feet indoors; it produces delicate-looking, feathery fronds.

C. tepejilote grows with a thick trunk ringed with "age joints" so you can determine its age. Usually can be found under lath for under ten dollars in mature state. Grows, indoors or out, to about nine feet with arching fronds nearly five feet long.

Use *Chamaedoreas* in bright, partially sunny locations. A bathroom with a skylight and eastern exposure is ideal, since all palms like high humidity. Kitchens also are good trial locations.

Basic care. Acclimation: None is required. All move indoors to bright, diffuse-light locations easily, provided humidity is raised around them for the first two to three weeks. **Soil:** A basic, fast-draining soil formula works best. Keep the mix barely moist through the summer and on the dry side through the winter. **Light:** Some summer sun is recommended and full winter sun is required. All will, however, thrive in bright, diffuse or reflected light. They can gradually be moved (over a period of months) to dimmer light where growth will slow to the proverbial snail's pace. **Temperature:** A range of 55° at night and 75° by day is best, but all will adapt to higher or lower ranges. **Humidity:** High humidity is part of the secret to growing healthy *Chamaedoreas* indoors. Twice-daily misting is needed in hot weather, and setting the palm on water-covered pebbles in a saucer or tray keeps the foliage attractive. **Fertilizer:** Feed with a complete fertilizer monthly from spring to fall, four to six months after purchase. **Propagation:** From seeds, or start with new, established plants.

Chamaedorea

Citrus

Citrus trees make attractive, unusual, fragrant, colorful — and inexpensive — indoor plants. You can take your pick of over twenty-five dwarf varieties (four to ten feet) of lemon, lime, orange, kumquat, tangelo—or virtually any citrus tree that bears fruit. Or choose a standard tree which could eventually take the roof off. Three of the best of the dwarfs to start with are *C. limonia* (lemon); *C. aurantifolia* (lime); and *C. taitensis* (orange). All three adapt well indoors if they're kept cool and given the care they need. You'll get, with very little effort, beautiful, aromatic flowers followed by colorful (but usually extremely tart) fruit. Even when a citrus tree is not in flower or fruit, it makes an impressive foliage plant with glossy leaves and appealing branch structure. If you want your tree to fruit indoors, you'll have to take the role of the bee and transfer pollen from the anther of one blossom to the stigma of another, which—oddly enough—is called hand pollina-

tion. Use either a small artist's brush or a wooden match that has been moistened to accomplish this. If you buy a citrus tree at the nursery, get one either in bud or in bloom and partially fruited. This guarantees you good health and floral display. Citrus trees (particularly lemon and orange) are highly susceptible to

Citrus

spider mites, which are exceedingly difficult to eradicate. Frequent misting helps some, since mites loathe moisture, but this is only a temporary preventive measure. When you buy, check for small, imperfect webs and apparently healthy blossoms which drop at the slightest touch. These are two indications of mite infestation. Pruning is almost always required to preserve a balanced, structurally attractive tree. Branches often grow out erratically and should be cut back while the tree is still young.

Use citrus trees in the kitchens of air-conditioned homes, where their fragrance and beauty make kitchen work a bit more bearable, or in any bright, cool spot. In mild weather, a month or two outdoors is very beneficial.

Basic care. Acclimation: None is needed, provided the plant is given a bright, cool location at the outset. **Soil:** All citrus plants need an acid soil formula kept well watered when the tree is in bloom or fruit, and on the dry side the rest of the year. Fast drainage is important, though, so add a little extra coarse builder's sand to the mix. **Light:** Very bright natural light, which means some summer sun, maximum winter sun (or blossoms may not appear), and diffuse light the rest of the year. **Temperature:** The cool range is best: 50° to 55° at night and 60° to 65° by day, though citrus plants can take both cooler and warmer ranges and thrive. **Humidity:** High humidity is best, particularly in hot weather and when the tree is in bloom or fruit. It may be necessary to irrigate every other day in summer. Mist frequently. **Fertilizer:** Feed with an acid fertilizer monthly, beginning when you acquire the tree, from spring through the fall. Citrus trees often suffer from iron chlorosis (yellowing foliage) brought on by frequent irrigations, which flush nutrients and trace elements out of the soil. At the first sign of yellowing, give the tree a dose of chelated iron additive. This should restore leaf tone within a day or two. **Propagation:** From cuttings in spring or from seeds.

Coleus

Common name: Painted-leaf plant
Nativity: Asia

Coleus is another of the colorful, inexpensive plants which is prized for its ability to brighten a dreary winter window. It is coming back strong as a desirable houseplant after years of being relegated to borders in summer gardens. Common coleus (*C. blumei*) comes in nature's full array of colorful leaf accents—red, wine, orange, yellow, salmon, green, etc. Leaves vary in length from half an inch to four inches and maximum height for the species is about three feet. With all varieties, one must be heartless about pinching out growing tips every three or four weeks. This keeps the plant full, bushy and growing vigorously. Be on guard against mealybug invasions. If a plant is severely invested, discard it and start with new plants. Because coleus foliage is sensitive to chemicals, pests can't be eradicated successfully by artificial methods without harming the plant. If the plant summers outdoors it may bloom. The best bargain in *Coleus* is flats purchased from the nursery in early spring, which means you'll have up to twenty-five plants to pot up in four-inch pots. These can be brought along rapidly with regular doses of high-nitrogen fertilizer and will make attractive, desirable gifts for friends and family. With flats, be particularly on guard against aphids and mealybugs. To encourage faster, larger growth, pinch out flower buds as they appear. Otherwise, the plants will concentrate their energies on floral production at the expense of foliage development.

Use coleus wherever a bright accent is desired, but this should be a sunny spot to preserve foliage color.

Basic care. Acclimation: None required. **Soil:** Basic soil mix with sand and horticultural charcoal (one cup each per gallon of potting medium), plus one tablespoon of ground limestone. Keep mix evenly moist spring to fall and barely moist the balance of the year. **Light:** Sun, winter and summer, helps retain brilliance of foliage. Will grow well in bright, diffuse light, however. **Temperature:** A range of 65° night and 80°+ day is recommended. **Humidity:** Average, but needs good ventilation when sitting in full sun. **Fertilizer:** Feed every two weeks spring through summer with a complete fertilizer diluted at half strength. **Propagation:** From stem cuttings and seeds.

Coleus

Cordyline stricta

Common names: Dracaena; palm lily
Nativity: Australia

One of the best bargains in outdoor plants, *C. stricta* has just about everything going for it—low price, fast growth, beauty, easy adaptability to indoor environments and self-propagation. Its characteristics are long (eight inches to two feet), sword-like, arching leaves and a delicate-looking but strong dracaena-like trunk. It closely resembles the costlier indoor status plant, *Dracaena marginata*, but is related to agave and yucca. In fact, those who've always wanted a *D. marginata* but have found the price too exorbitant would do well to consider *C. stricta* as an inexpensive but just as appealing alternative. Outdoors, it grows to fourteen feet and produces purplish flower clusters in spring; indoors, eight feet is average and we have yet to see blooms appear on our specimens, some of which are ten years old. The plant has what most consider an appealing habit of sacrificing lower leaves in favor of greater top growth and more trunk so that, eventually, it takes on the appearance of a graceful tree crowned with a burst of foliage. Suckers or offsets often appear any time of year, but usually in the spring; and these can be used to increase your stock or left to produce a nice display of plants of staggered heights. Damaged plants can be cut back at any point and, in a matter of weeks, will replace old foliage with vigorous new growth.

Use *C. stricta* virtually anywhere. It makes an appealing entry plant, particularly as it attains height.

Basic care. Acclimation: None is required; the plant adjusts to indoor environments almost overnight. **Soil:** Basic soil mix should be kept barely moist. **Light:** Maximum light seems to yield the best results, though the plant can take sun through an east window or curtain-filtered sun through west windows. The plant will grow well in less intense illumination—five feet from a north window, for example. This also often intensifies the coloring of the foliage, while brighter light causes the foliage to pale slightly. **Temperature:** In the warm range of 60° to 65° at night and 75° to 85° by day, with good ventilation. **Humidity:** Average, but daily misting keeps the foliage attractive and healthy. **Fertilizer:** Begin feeding monthly with a complete fertilizer through the fall four to six months after purchase. **Propagation:** Offsets can be easily rooted in sand or moss any time of the year. The plant also responds well to air layering.

NOTE: Field-grown specimens are often infested with mealy bugs. If infestation isn't too severe, you can remove them with an alcohol-soaked cotton swab. Isolate an infested plant until the pests have been eradicated. Avoid heavily pest-ridden plants.

Cordyline stricta

Cordyline terminalis

Common name: Baby Ti
Nativity: Hawaii

In the South Sea islands, *C. terminalis* grows to ten feet and its durable leaves, which grow to nearly three feet in length, are the natives' source of roof thatching and hula skirt material. Two common varieties are *C. terminalis bicolor*, which is green and pink, and *C. terminalis tricolor*, whose foliage is striped with shades of red, pink and white. In most sections of the United States, the Ti plant is known only as a stem section, or "log." But, in temperate areas, *C. terminalis* is available in cans for landscaping use. These mature specimens can grow to five or six feet indoors, if cultivated properly. Actually, the Ti is tough and tolerant of abuse, provided it gets the sunlight and high humidity it prefers. Damaged plants can be air layered or cut back and will recover nicely, sprouting vigorously below the cut. If you can only find *C. terminalis* as a four-inch log, which will probably be the case in northern portions of the country, start with two logs (occasionally, one may not sprout) imbedded to a depth of half an inch in a 50-50 mixture of peat moss and sharp builder's sand, which is kept continually moist. Plantlets, which sprout from dormant "eyes," will appear faster if the container is kept warm and covered with polyethylene. (Ventilate for a few minutes daily to prevent mold and mildew.) When the plantlets are about four inches long, remove them close to the log with a sharp knife or single-edged razor blade and root them in moist sand. Once a good root structure has developed, they can be potted up in four-inch pots and given the same care as established plants.

Use *C. terminalis* in a sunny kitchen or bathroom. It likes the steam and warmth both locations provide.

Basic care. Acclimation: None required. **Soil:** A basic mix with extra sand and two tablespoons of limestone to a gallon of potting medium. Keep the soil evenly moist through the fall and almost dry during the winter months. **Light:** Needs lots of summer sun (with good ventilation) to intensify and preserve the bold color of its foliage, but will survive in bright, diffuse to medium light. **Temperature:** Prefers the warm range of its homeland—68° to 70° at night, 78° to 85° during the day. Plant will adjust to normal interior

ranges, either cooler or warmer. **Humidity:** Deteriorates in anything but high humidity. Needs misting twice a day in hot weather or a tray underneath of water-covered pebbles. **Fertilizer:** Feed monthly from spring to fall with a complete fertilizer diluted to half strength. **Propagation:** Propagate by air layering or with stem cuttings.

Cordyline terminalis

Corynocarpus laevigatus

Common name: New Zealand laurel
Nativity: New Zealand

An obscure but desirable indoor-outdoor specimen that does best if allowed to summer outdoors and is wintered indoors, but will eventually adjust to a year-round interior environment. In its native country, *C. laevigatus* grows to impressive heights—thirty feet or more—but the best one can hope for indoors is a modest six or, perhaps, seven feet. It can be kept

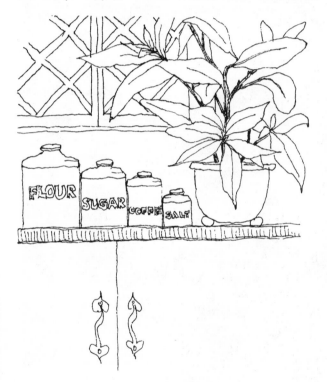

shrubby as a juvenile specimen by topping off. Its attractiveness is in its foliage which is oblong, deep green and glossy and is about five to six inches long and two inches wide. It does flower outdoors, but it is doubtful that it will do so inside. Flowers are followed by orange fruit which is *deadly poison*. Because of this, those with small children or gnawing puppies in the family might do well to pass on *C. laevigatus* either as an indoor *or* an outdoor plant.

Use *C. laevigatus* in a bright, sunny, well-ventilated spot, such as a kitchen, atrium or sunporch.

Basic care. Acclimation: Requires the full adaptation period outlined for sun-loving plants. Even after plant has been acclimated, it does best if treated as an indoor-outdoor plant, unless raised from a seedling or juvenile. **Soil:** Basic mix with extra sand. Keep soil barely moist. **Light:** Some summer sun is beneficial and full, maximum winter sun is recommended. Can survive in bright, diffuse light. **Temperature:** Adapts to the typical interior ranges, but needs good ventilation when the temperature rises above 75°. Does well in cooler levels than most traditional houseplants. **Humidity:** Average. A daily misting in warm weather is helpful. **Fertilizer:** After six months, feed from spring to fall with a complete fertilizer at full strength. **Propagation:** From seeds.

Corynocarpus laevigatus

Crassula

Nativity: South Africa and other locales

Three members of the *Crassulaceae* (cras-you-LAY'see-ee) family achieve size substantial enough to rank them as large: *C. arborescens*, or silver dollar; *C. argentea*, or jade tree; and *C. falcata*. As succulents, they are easy-care houseplants that require very little fussing over, and they adapt well to our traditionally overheated American homes. All three cultivars listed above can be acquired inexpensively in substantial size as field-grown specimens in temperate areas of the United States.

C. arborescens tends to be shrubby, with foliage that resembles the popular jade tree, except that the leaves are more noticeably edged in red and also are speckled with red. Older plants produce striking, star-shaped white flowers in late summer, but the plant may not bloom indoors. *C. arborescens* slowly grows to about three feet.

C. argentea is no stranger indoors, but is most familiar as a small dish garden or seed-

Crassula

ling plant. Larger, more mature plants make much more impressive and attractive plants, with interesting branch structures and thick, stout trunks. *C. argentea* grows easily indoors to five feet, often higher, but is a slow grower. Start with the largest specimen you can find. Although the jade tree blooms in late fall, it may not produce its white floral display indoors unless growing conditions are ideal.

C. falcata, another popular dish-garden plant, is really attractive in its mature state. Its thick gray-green, sickle-shaped leaves grow compactly on branches, and as a bonus, it blooms with clusters of bright red flowers in late summer. *C. falcata*, under optimum conditions, can grow four feet high with a spread as wide.

Use all three plants where you want a splash of color. All three do well in a typical sunny kitchen situation.

Basic care. Acclimation: None is required. Even *Crassula* plants that have grown in an outdoor garden for years can be carefully uprooted, potted up, and brought indoors, where they'll continue to thrive. **Soil:** To a gallon of basic soil mix, add an extra cup of sharp builder's sand and one tablespoon of limestone. Also, mix two tablespoons of steamed bonemeal in the bottom layer of soil in the pot. Keep the soil on the dry side. Water thoroughly, then let the soil dry to a depth of two inches before irrigating again. **Light:** Some summer sun and full winter sun keep these succulents happy and encourages them to bloom. All will survive with only bright, diffuse light. **Temperature:** A night temperature of 55° to 60° and a daytime level of 65° to 75° is best. All three plants will adapt to the 50° to 80° range. **Humidity:** Average. **Propagation:** From leaf or stem cuttings easily rooted in sand any time of year. (Bury only the roots when you pot up or the cutting may rot.)

Dizygotheca elegantissima

Common names: Aralia elegantissima; marijuana plant; threadleaf
Nativity: New Hebrides

In sheltered gardens in California and Florida, this attractive plant grows into a delicate-looking, slender-trunked tree eight to ten feet tall. These same field-grown specimens can be brought directly from the nursery indoors and will reach the same impressive size, depending upon the height of your ceiling.

As a juvenile plant, the rough, dun-colored stem may be covered with flat palmate fans of seven to ten deep green serrated leaves. Often, as the plant matures, the lower leaves are dropped and the plant takes on the appearance of a tree, carrying the fans aloft on slender trunks. If the proper balance of soil moisture content and soil aridity is not maintained, the plant will drop leaves by the dozens. If this occurs, the stem can be cut back and will soon produce new foliage. This may also encourage attractive branching. However, it isn't necessary to sacrifice stem height to stimulate refoliation. Simply let the plant recover on its own. Be especially alert for scale infestation with field-grown *D. elegantissima*. *D. elegantissima* is usually found under lath at the nursery in both gallon and five gallon cans. If you want a bold, focal-point plant immediately, buy two five-gallon specimens and pot them up together. If you're the patient type, buy four one-gallon plants and pot them up in a single container. In four or five years, you'll have a very becoming display of plants six to seven feet tall. If you opt for the latter method, remember to pinch out new growth from time to time to force branching.

Use *D. elegantissima* wherever you can provide warmth and good light. Definitely not fond of dark corners.

Basic care. Acclimation: None required, even with mature specimens. **Soil:** Basic soil mix with some sand, kept evenly moist in spring and summer and barely moist the rest of the year. **Light:** Needs bright, diffuse light the year around. Can take full winter sun. Some can adapt to an hour or two of direct summer sun, with adequate ventilation. **Temperature:** On the warm side—65° at night and 80° during the day—but adapts to most normal interior levels. **Humidity:** Average. Mist often to discourage spider mites and to freshen foliage. **Fertilizer:** Feed monthly from spring to fall with a complete fertilizer diluted at half strength. **Propagation:** From hardwood cuttings.

Dizygotheca elegantissima

Euphorbia splendens

Common names: E. Milii; Crown of Thorns
Nativity: Madagascar

It's hard to believe that the delicate Christmas flower, poinsettia, is a member of the same family as this barbed, wicked-looking little guy. Although *E. splendens* is densely studded with potentially punishing spikes, it is a durable, colorful and unusual specimen which can be trained on a frame or wire as a climber

or left to its own wandering devices. It grows into a multi-branched shrub about three feet high and carries a few bright green leaves near the tips of its branches. These usually fall if the plant becomes excessively dry. If given good light, it retains a few quarter-inch red bracts at the ends of its branches. This is not a plant you want to handle often, so pick a permanent location when you bring it home—a spot out of the general flow of traffic, for obvious reasons.

Use Crown of Thorns wherever you want an unusual accent, but this must be a sunny, partially sunny, or bright, diffuse light situation.

Basic care. Acclimation: None. Goes from the nursery to a sun-drenched window without a struggle. **Soil:** A basic mix with extra sand and two tablespoons of ground limestone to a gallon of potting medium. Keep slightly dry through the summer, but never let the soil completely dry out. In winter, cut back to just enough water to keep the plant alive. **Light:** Prefers a few hours of direct summer sun daily . . . full winter sun . . . or bright, diffuse light year round. In dim light, the red bracts die back. **Temperature:** A pushover for a warm, cozy environment. A range of 65° at night and 80° during the day is ideal. A cold, drafty spot causes the leaves to fall. **Humidity:** Low. Mist occasionally to discourage spiders. **Fertilizer:** Feed every two months from spring to fall with a complete fertilizer diluted at half strength. **Propagation:** From stem cuttings which have callused by "resting" for five to eight days.

Euphorbia splendens (Crown of thorns)

Fatshedera lizei

Common names: Ivy tree; botanical wonder
Nativity: (See below)

F. *lizei* is called "botanical wonder" because it is a freak of nature. It is the result of an accidental cross between Moser's Japanese fatsia (*Fatsia japonica moserii*) and Irish ivy (*Hedera helix hibernica*) in a French nursery at the turn of the century, hence the name (*fats*, for fatsia + hedera). The plant has retained some of the

features of both parents. Its foliage (six-inch-wide leaves) has the lobed characteristics of *F. japonica* and can be trained as a shrub (three feet is an average height). It also has a natural tendency to vine like ivy. To encourage massing and branching, pinch out the growing tips twice a year. Train stems while they're still green and pliable to conform to the shape or growth pattern you desire. *F. lizei* can be pruned back hard and will produce vigorous new growth rapidly. The variety *variegata*, which has leaves edged in white, is a slow grower and is not as easy as *F. lizei*.

Use the plant virtually anywhere. Although it thrives in bright natural light, you may be able, as others have, to use it to brighten a dimly lit corner where a little color is appreciated.

Basic care. Acclimation: As a shade-lover, *F. lizei* goes directly indoors without an outdoor acclimation period, but keep humidity high around the plant for the first two weeks. Try it initially in an east or north window. If it continues to flourish, move it to the spot where you'd like to keep it permanently. **Soil:** A basic planting mix with one tablespoon of limestone added to a gallon of soil is ideal for *F. lizei*. Keep it evenly moist and give it lots of water on hot "dog days." **Light:** A bright window location with no direct sun produces the best specimens, but the plant can adapt to very low light levels. It will probably drop some leaves if the light is inadequate, so watch for this as an indicator. **Temperature:** The plant prefers a cool environment, 40° to 55° at night and 65° to 70° by day, but should adapt readily to other levels. **Humidity:** Average humidity. It responds well to frequent misting on hot days, which also discourages the spider mites that frequently plague this plant. **Fertilizer:** After four to six months, feed monthly from spring to fall with a complete fertilizer. **Propagation:** Take stem cuttings or air layer at any time of year; in spring the results are quicker.

Fatshedera lizei

Fatsia japonica

Common names: Japanese aralia or fatsia; Aralia sieboldii
Nativity: Japan

Fatsia is a striking foliage plant that is just now gaining a foothold as a houseplant after years of use as an outdoor entry or shade landscaping accent. It has some of the features of the popular shefflera—stout woody trunk and

glossy, deeply cut leaves which are often fifteen inches across. It is a faster grower than shefflera. Outdoors it can reach eight feet; indoors, five feet is average. If grown in good light, it produces tiny panicles of delicate white flowers which are followed by black berries. To encourage larger leaf development, unless you want to propagate from seed, these flowers should be pinched off as soon as they appear. A plant that has weather-damaged or sun-damaged foliage can be cut back as far

down the stem as you like in early spring, which is also a method of keeping it short but fuller. In a matter of weeks you'll have an explosion of fresh, new foliage.

Use *Fatsia japonica* in a cool corner that gets good light, or on an enclosed sun porch. Hot spots or sunny windows are *verboten*. It wilts in overheated, unventilated interiors.

Basic care. Acclimation: Fatsia goes without a whimper from the nursery to your interior, if you can provide a cool niche and bright, diffuse light. Keep it well watered for a couple of weeks after moving it inside. **Soil:** Give it a basic soil that is kept evenly moist. If leaves begin to sag even with high humidity, increase water volume or frequency of irrigation. It can often handle more water than most other plants, especially when it's grown indoors. **Light:** The plant can take full winter sun in most locales, but yellowing or browning foliage may indicate it's getting a sunburn. It does quite well the year around with bright, diffuse light. **Temperature:** While it can take summer sun and hot air temperatures outdoors, it flags and deteriorates in an overheated interior. The cool range of 50° to 55° at night and 65° to 75° by day—or even cooler—produces the best specimens. **Humidity:** Average humidity. Mist frequently on hot summer days. **Fertilizer:** Feed every month with a complete dilute fertilizer from early spring to late fall beginning four months after acquisition of the plant. **Propagation:** Take suckers which the plant produces near its base. If you let the plant go to seed, you can harvest these when they've browned off in late fall or early winter.

Fatsia japonica

Feijoa sellowiana

Common name: Pineapple guava
Nativity: Brazil

Like the cereal-selling, pine tree-eating gentleman from videoland said, "Many parts are edible." Mr. G would love this tree. Its attractive oval foliage (about three inches long at maturity) is deep glossy green with a white midrib on top and covered with a faint silver fuzz underneath. It's a natural spreader and responds well to pruning and shaping in late spring. Cutting back new growth helps create a shrubbier specimen. Outdoors, it may grow to twenty or more feet with an equal spread. *Feijoas* (fay·SHOW'uh) bloom outdoors in early spring (may bloom earlier indoors) producing beautiful white, cup-shaped flowers which have prominent red stamens. These must be hand-pollinated or the plant won't fruit. Two varieties which require cross-pollination, and should be avoided for this reason unless you want only foliage, are: *F. s. 'Choceana'* and *F. s. 'Superba.'* The petals of the flowers are edible and make a colorful and tasty addition to fresh fruit salads or they can be used for garnishing many culinary dishes. Fruits appear if pollination was successful soon after and ripen in about four months. Indoors, they may not be as large as those produced in a natural environment, ranging anywhere from two to four inches. The fruit itself is oval, dull green and may have a slightly crimson flush. It is filled inside with a soft, bland pulp that has some of the flavor overtone of pineapple, hence the common name.

Use *F. sellowiana* in any sunny location which can be kept cool at night.

Basic care. Acclimation: None required, provided you can give the plant immediately a location which gets good, direct sun for a few hours daily, with ventilation.

Soil: A basic soil mix kept on the dry side. Let the soil dry out between irrigations to a depth of one and a half to two inches. **Light:** Requires a few hours of direct sun daily to thrive, but will survive in bright, diffuse light. Fails in dim light. **Temperature:** Prefers a night level around 50° or 55° and a day level of 65° to 70°. As with most plants, you may be able to adapt it to other ranges, with time and patience. Good ventilation is needed with higher temperatures. **Humidity:** Average. A daily misting through the hot summer days is beneficial. **Fertilizer:** Feed every two months from spring to fall with a complete fertilizer diluted at half strength. **Propagation:** Propagate from seeds, cuttings or by air layering.

Feijoa sellowiana

Ficus benjamina

Common names: Weeping Chinese banyan; weeping fig
Nativity: Malaya, India

Without a doubt, *F. benjamina* is one of the most desirable, sought after plants for indoor cultivation, ranking with its brother, *F. lyrata* (fiddle-leaf fig), in popularity and inflated price.

Its beauty comes from a fawn-colored, birch-like trunk and many-twigged, drooping branches densely covered with two-inch to three-inch-long ovate leaves of deep, glossy green. Outdoors, it can grow to thirty-five feet; indoors, most are kept off the ceiling by selective pruning of top growth, which also encourages branching. If given proper care and feeding, it is a fast grower, adding eight to ten inches a year. Frankly, *F. benjamina* is rarely available in most parts of the country, and when it is the price is usually outrageous. In many outlets in California, field-grown speci-

mens are offered periodically at irresistible prices—three-foot trees in one-gallon cans for under four dollars and five-foot trees in five-gallon cans for about sixteen dollars.

Use *F. benjamina* as the focal point in a bright, partially sunny window. It also does well in kitchens which are light and airy.

Basic care. Acclimation: Field-grown specimens from the nursery require the full acclimation cycle and sometimes never really adapt satisfactorily. But even greenhouse-grown benjaminas often go through phases of leaf yellowing and leaf loss once they're moved from a controlled environment to an over-heated, low-humidity interior. See the chapter on acclimating outdoor plants for detailed instructions on adapting sun-loving plants. **Soil:** A basic soil mix works well. Keep it barely moist, or more specifically, a little on the dry side. **Light:** It needs all the winter sun it can get and may be able to handle direct summer sun from an east window exposure. If leaves become sunburned, a thin curtain between the plant and the window is sufficient protection. Benjaminas are definitely not plants for dark corners. Field-grown specimens, in particular, seem to demand maximum light. Greenhouse-grown specimens can often survive totally on artificial (florescent) illumination. **Temperature:** Optimum temperature levels are 65° to 70° at night and 75° to 80° by day, but acclimated field-grown specimens seem to respond better to cooler ranges. **Humidity:** High humidity the year around is beneficial. Frequent misting helps discourage red spider mites, which are inordinately fond of benjaminas. **Fertilizer:** Feed monthly with a complete fertilizer from spring to fall beginning four to six months after purchase. **Propagation:** By air layering in early spring.

Ficus benjamina

Ficus elastica decora

Common names: Rubber plant; rubber tree
Nativity: India, Malaya

In most of the country, the rubber tree is known only as a houseplant. As such, its popularity has waxed and waned. Some "plant snobs" wouldn't have a *F. e. decora* in their homes if you gave them one simply because "just everyone has that tatty old thing." It may not have status, but we feel the rubber tree is a noble and worthy specimen. It is virtually indestructible, and if you *do* hack it to pieces, you can propagate them and start all over. In California and along the Gulf Coast to Florida, *F. e. decora* is sold as a landscaping plant for sheltered overhangs, tunnels, and patios. We find these field-grown versions ideal for indoor cultivation. They're often more mature than the greenhouse-grown variety which sells for four to five dollars, and they often have an attractive branch structure, which as the plant attains height shows in miniature what this hundred-foot tropical giant looks like in its native habitat. Best of all, the price is well under ten dollars for a beautiful specimen in a five-gallon can. *F. e. decora* will drop its lower leaves no matter what you do to frustrate this annoying habit. You may try cutting growing tips, holding back water and fertilizer, talking to it—nothing works. This is why air layering is eventually necessary with greenhouse-grown rubber trees. But multi-branched field-grown specimens may not require air layering. The naked trunk, carrying aloft branches of leaves, is the natural condition and makes an attractive display. There is no limit to the size a rubber tree can reach indoors, other than the height of your ceiling. Its bold oval leaves unfurl from a red leaf sheath which dies and drops off after releasing the new leaf. If a sheath has only partially opened and remains that way over two weeks, you should gently pull it away and release the leaf manually to prevent the leaf from rotting. Sometimes the sheath gets distracted and forgets to finish its job.

Use *F. e. decora* anywhere you can provide warmth and bright light. As the plant isn't sensitive to gas, in our experience, a kitchen, which is usually the warmest spot in the house, is ideal.

Basic care. Acclimation: Field-grown trees should be kept for a week to ten days in the coldest spot in the house with very little light. Withhold water but keep the leaves misted. Then, when you bring it out into the light and give it water, you should get a burst of vigorous growth. **Soil:** A basic mix should be kept on the dry side. **Light:** Maximum diffuse light, but no summer sun. The plant can take winter sun in most areas. **Temperature:** The plant needs warmth—not under 60° at night and not over 80° by day. **Humidity:** Average, and high in summer. A daily misting and weekly washing of the broad, dust-catching leaves are beneficial. **Fertilizer:** Start feeding monthly from spring to fall with a complete fertilizer four months after purchase. **Propagation:** Air layering is the traditional propagation technique.

NOTE: All of the above are the ideal cultivation procedures, but rubber trees are so determined to survive they not only live but thrive in the most primitive conditions and inept hands. We've seen them doing splendidly in almost total darkness indoors; on cold, unheated sunporches; and in hot, unventilated homes. Usually the plants are also coping bravely with daily drenchings from owners who thought the plants could be induced to swim, in addition to all their other talents. In short, this is the plant for indoor gardeners who are all thumbs—none of which is green.

Ficus elastica decora

Ficus retusa nitida

Common name: Indian laurel
Nativity: Malaya

Another member of the aristocratic ficus (fig) family, *F.r.nitida* is seldom tried indoors but adjusts well in a warm, brightly illuminated location. Its trunk is dun-colored and carries a thick mass of upright branches that can be selectively pruned to induce the tree to grow into many different shapes. Its deep green, oval leaves at maturity are three to four inches long and three-quarters of an inch to one inch wide. *F.r.nitida* grows to more than fifteen feet outdoors, but seven feet is average indoors. Unfortunately, field-grown nitidas are frequently infested with a difficult-to-eradicate pest—

thrips—which stipple new leaves. Leaf surfaces become whitened (by "white blast," now an obsolete term) and flecked as the eggs of thrips, which have been laid in the leaf, hatch into hungry nymphs in a single week and immediately begin to suck the sap from the tree. An infested nitida usually has new foliage that

Ficus retusa nitida

is spotted brown or brown and red with some leaves curled. The best way to cope with thrips is to use a systemic poison in the soil, and in this case a second application in two weeks may be necessary. We have occasionally broken our rule of never buying a pest-infested plant in the case of nitidas, since they are often unavailable as inexpensive field-grown specimens *without* thrips. We've been successful in confining the thrips to the tree we've acquired by isolating it and beginning immediate treatment.

Use *F. r. nitida* in any bright location. Two trees in one pot can be used effectively as a privacy screen in tall, narrow windows, but not in west windows during the summer.

Basic care. Acclimation: Nitidas are considerably easier to acclimate than field-grown *F. benjaminas*. Go through the entire cycle recommended for sun-loving plants outlined in the chapter on adapting outdoor plants to indoor life. **Soil:** Basic soil mix should be kept on the dry side. Let the soil dry out to a depth of two inches before irrigating again. **Light:** The plant should have maximum light, which means full sun from an east window or diffuse light from a west window covered with a thin curtain. A north or south window location may provide sufficient light. If new foliage development slows, try a brighter spot. **Temperature:** Keep the temperature on the warm side—in the mid-sixties at night, in the high seventies to low eighties during the day, but, especially in the higher ranges, provide good ventilation. **Humidity:** High humidity, except during cold weather, is recommended for best results. **Fertilizer:** Feed with a complete fertilizer bi-monthly from spring to fall beginning four to six months after purchase. **Propagation:** Air layering works well and may be necessary as nitidas begin to touch the ceiling.

Ficus roxburghii

Nativity: India

F. *roxburghii* is rarely tried indoors because it is briefly deciduous. Its evergreen Australian cousin, F. *rubiginosa*, or rustyleaf fig, is more commonly cultivated for interior use. F. *roxburghii* is such a bold, beautiful plant it's well worth the short period of naked branches just to have it around the rest of the year. It may be that in some years the foliage will not drop. The change from an environment of rising and falling temperatures to one of more or less consistently even temperatures the year around, is the reason for this phenomenon. This is not a plant for tiny apartments—it requires a great deal of room as it matures, often attaining a height and width of seven feet, maybe even ten feet. Pruning back helps keep it manageable and trains it into an attractive tree. Although it produces large figs in clusters, its primary appeal is its large oval leaves (fourteen to sixteen inches across) which are maroon when new but change into a vibrant green at maturity.

Use F. *roxburghii* as a focal-point plant or to divide or define a space. Its high light requirement limits your choice of location to some extent, and its size may hamper you even more.

Basic care. Acclimation: In the spring, select juvenile plants under lath at the nursery. These are easier to adapt since they are already accustomed to shade and can make the transition to an indoor location without too much difficulty. Move newly potted plants to a window which gets bright, diffuse light and provide high humidity and good air circulation. A tray of water-covered pebbles helps maintain a beneficial microclimate during the acclimation period. Pruning back some of the foliage will help the plant through the transition period. **Soil:** Basic soil mix should be kept barely moist; it needs good drainage. **Light:** Full winter sun is best, or the plant may do well all year with bright, diffuse light. **Temperature:** A range of 60° to 65° at night and 70° to 75° by day produces good results. **Humidity:** A little higher than most. Misting twice a day is necessary in hot weather, along with good ventilation; daily misting in winter when the heater dries out the air helps. **Fertilizer:** The plant responds well to monthly feeding with a complete fertilizer from spring to late fall beginning four to six months after purchase. **Propagation:** From cuttings in spring.

Ficus roxburghii

Ficus rubiginosa variegata

Common name: Miniature rubber tree
Nativity: Australia

The interesting feature of *F. r. variegata* which makes it an unusual and desirable specimen is the foliage. On a good specimen, half the leaves will be splotched with creamy markings on the edges and green in the center, the other half will be completely green, giving the appearance of two different plants growing on the same rootstock. In its native Queensland, *F. rubiginosa* grows to sixty feet producing ovate leaves five inches long. *F. r. variegata*, a cultivar, doesn't achieve this kind of height but grows into an impressive tree, under ideal conditions. This is a difficult specimen for novices to grow outside a greenhouse, especially when tried in an overheated, unventilated living room. It requires high humidity to thrive. But, its striking foliage should make it worth the gamble. *F. rubiginosa*, or "rustyleaf fig," is usually available as a seedling tree with a single trunk. As it matures, several trunks may develop. Its thick foliage is about four to five inches long, vibrant green on top and usually rust-colored and fuzzy underneath. It needs considerably more sun than *F. r. variegata*, but calls for similar care.

Use *F. r. variegata* wherever you can provide warmth, good light and high humidity. A modern kitchen or bath should fill the plant's requirements.

Basic care. Acclimation: None required. **Soil:** A basic soil mix kept evenly moist is recommended. Add extra sand for good drainage. **Light:** Bright, diffuse light in summer; full sun in winter. Can survive in

less intense illumination. **Temperature:** The warm range is best—65° at night and 80° by day—but will adapt to most interior levels. **Humidity:** High humidity is required to grow this plant successfully. A tray of water-covered pebbles under the plant will do the job, or twice-daily misting in warm weather. Daily misting helps, also, in winter to counteract the hot, dry air created by central heating. **Fertilizer:** After four months, from spring through summer, feed monthly with a complete fertilizer diluted at half strength. **Propagation:** By air layering.

Ficus rubiginosa variegata (Rubber tree)

Fortunella margarita

Common name: Nagami kumquat
Nativity: China

This Chinese exotic produces orange one-inch fruits with a tart, edible rind frequently used to make a tasty marmalade. The white flowers which precede the fruit in spring and early summer perfume the air with an enchant-

ing orange-blossom aroma. If acquired as a tree growing on original roots, it grows to twenty-five feet outdoors, but averages only four or five indoors—unless it is given precisely the right care, which is seldom achieved outside the greenhouse. If purchased as a tree on dwarf rootstock, it takes on the appearance of a shrubby tree and reaches a maximum height of about three feet indoors. The foliage alone

makes it sufficiently appealing, whether it blooms and fruits or not. Leaves are dark, glossy green, oval, and about three inches long at maturity.

Use *F. margarita* in any bright, diffuse-light situation where it can be kept cool at night and slightly warmer during the day. It does well in air-conditioned environments with good light.

Basic care. Acclimation: Established field-grown specimens on standard rootstock may pose some problems in overheated interiors. Keep humidity high if foliage begins to dry or drop. This will probably occur, if it's going to, in the first two weeks. Seedlings and dwarfs adjust quite well without any fuss. **Soil:** An acid soil mix kept barely moist when tree is in flower or fruit, and slightly dry the rest of the year, is recommended. **Light:** The plant can use some direct summer sun, preferably from an eastern exposure. Full winter sun is beneficial, but, as a minimum requirement, give it bright, diffuse light the year around. **Temperature:** The plant prefers a cool nighttime temperature around 50°, and 70° to 75° during the day, though it tolerates cooler daytime levels. **Humidity:** It can use daily misting in hot weather and likes to have its leaves bathed once a week in winter. **Fertilizer:** Feed with an acid fertilizer every two months from spring to fall. **Propagation:** From stem cuttings and seeds, or start with new plants from the nursery.

Fortunella margarita

Ixora javanica

Common names: Jungle geranium; jungle flame
Nativity: Java and the East Indies

For those who want a small (rarely exceeds two feet indoors) attractive plant that blooms, for a sunny situation, this striking native of the Indies should fill the bill. Its elongated, leathery, emerald-green foliage, which is crimson until

fully matured, is about four inches long and is attractive enough in itself. But, with regular doses of sun, you'll also get clusters of waxy, tangerine flowers which account for the plant's common names. The blooms, alas, are short lived, but repeat annually. As with most plants,

pinching new growth periodically encourages fullness and larger foliage. *Ixora coccinea* has been around for decades and is used in a variety of landscaping applications in temperate areas around the world. Its bright red tubular flowers account for its common designation—"flame-of-the-woods." Established plants found at the nursery may be harder to acclimate than some of the newer hybrids which are tolerant of lower light levels. One of these is *I. "Frances Perry,"* which throws vibrant yellow flowers and can get by on filtered sun. Culture requirements for both are the same as for I. javanica, if you start with immature plants.

Use *Ixora* in a warm, sunny kitchen, living room or bath. Cool nooks or drafty spots are not appreciated by the plant, and it will show its displeasure by dropping leaves or going into dormancy.

Basic care. Acclimation: None required. **Soil:** A basic mix with extra sand and charcoal kept evenly moist, but never soggy. **Light:** Needs some summer sun, maximum winter sun and—as a minimum requirement—bright, diffuse light year-round. Will tolerate lower light levels, but will not perform well in dim places. **Temperature:** Keep *I. javanica* warm and cozy—65° at night and 80°+ by day (with good ventilation). **Humidity:** High in summer and average the rest of the year. **Fertilizer:** Feed monthly from early spring to fall with a complete fertilizer diluted at half strength. **Propagation:** Cuttings taken in spring will root rapidly.

Ixora javanica

Kalanchoe

Common name: Various, depending upon species
Nativity: Madagascar and Africa

Kalanchoes (kal-AN′-koe-ee) are durable, succulent plants which are prized for their interesting foliage characteristics and their bonus of blooms in midwinter.

K. beharensis (Kitchingia mandrakensis), commonly called the "felt plant," can grow to five feet and carry six or eight pairs of felt-covered, lance-shaped leaves.

K. blossfeldiana usually doesn't exceed two feet in height and has fleshy, deep-green leaves accented with red. Flowers are produced in clusters and run the color range from yellow to red, depending upon the hybrid.

K. laciniata grows to about four feet and produces four-inch-long leaves tinged green or red and clusters of yellow or red flowers.

K. tomentosa, or "panda plant," may reach two feet in height. Its fleshy leaves are often spotted brown and are covered with a thick mass of white, fuzz-like hair.

Use Kalanchoes in any sunny situation where winter color will be appreciated.

Basic care. Acclimation: None required. **Soil:** Start with a basic mix and add one cup of horticultural charcoal, two cups of sand and one tablespoon of ground limestone to a gallon of potting medium. Keep soil on the dry side. Kalanchoes are succulent and require very little moisture in the soil between irrigations. **Light:** Summer and winter sun produces best results, but all will thrive in bright, diffuse light. To promote winter bloom, cut down on light from late fall on—ten hours of light per day maximum. **Temperature:** Anything in the range of 50° at night and 75° by day is acceptable. **Humidity:** Low. Excessive moisture will promote mildew. **Fertilizer:** Feed every three months with a complete fertilizer diluted at half strength. **Propagation:** Propagate at any time from leaf or stem cuttings, or take offsets from some varieties.

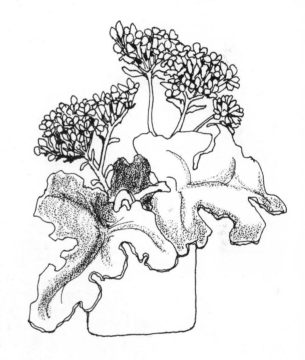

Kalanchoe in bloom

Laurus nobilis

Common names: Sweet bay; Grecian laurel
Nativity: Mediterranean

After an illustrious background as a source of crowns for ancient Greek and Roman heroes and nobility, and a continuing career as a flavor enhancer for many culinary dishes, the laurel has come into its own as an attractive houseplant for cool interior locations. In the seedling stage, it grows with a single stem, but

as it matures, it develops several trunks and produces masses of thick foliage—aromatic, dark-green, leathery leaves an inch wide and

two to four inches long. Older specimens bloom with tiny yellow flowers, which are followed by one-inch-long black berries. It responds well to selective pruning and shaping, and as a slow grower, it can be kept in the same container for years. Annual top dressing adds needed nutrients to the old soil. Outdoors, it grows to forty feet or more and indoors the ceiling's the limit, if you start with a specimen in a five-gallon can.

Use *L. nobilis* in any cool, brightly illuminated location. An entry is ideal, since it is tolerant of drafts. The plant does well in any air-conditioned interior which gets good light.

Basic care. Acclimation: Field-grown specimens require the full adaptation period, as outlined for sun-loving plants in the chapter on acclimating outdoor plants. Seedlings can usually adapt without any specialized treatment. Keep the plant cool and withhold water for the first two weeks after you bring it indoors. **Soil:** A basic soil mix with extra sand is recommended. Keep the mix just barely moist. Let the top soil dry out to a depth of one inch before irrigating again. **Light:** The plant can take some summer sun and needs full winter sun, but it will survive the year around in bright, diffuse light, though it fails in dark corners. **Temperature:** The coolest possible range —40° to 50° at night and under 65° during the day—is recommended, though it may adapt to slightly higher levels in time. Young seedlings usually accept normal household ranges easily. **Humidity:** Average. Mist foliage occasionally to remove dust. **Fertilizer:** Feed monthly from April through July with a complete fertilizer diluted to half strength. **Propagation:** By cuttings or air layering. Seeds may be sown and germinated, if you're the patient type.

Laurus nobilis

Ligustrum lucidum 'Texanum'

Common names: Texas privet; waxleaf privet
Nativity: Japan

Rarely tried indoors, the waxleaf privet makes a delightful and easily adaptable shrub. As a houseplant, it can be encouraged to grow into a tree six to seven feet tall simply by letting it "do its thing," or it can be kept dense, short and shrub-like by selective pruning. As a matter of fact, its branches and foliage respond well to trimming and shaping into almost any configuration you desire. Outdoors it is primarily used as a thick, bushy hedge. Its shiny, leathery leaves are tough and help it take on the "horrors" of indoor life (drafts; hot, dry air; etc.) and go right on thriving magnificently. Although it blooms in a profusion of white flowers in spring, it—like most other traditional outdoor plants—may not do so indoors, but you can never tell. The flowers are followed by small black berries which are the seeds of the species and usually self-sow outdoors.

Use *L. l. 'Texanum'* in any bright location. It adapts as easily in kitchens as living rooms and it can be trained and used as a privacy screen, in lieu of drapes or shades.

Basic care. Acclimation: Seedlings require no acclimation period. Move the plant immediately into a bright, partially sunny location and keep humidity high for the first two weeks. **Soil:** A basic mix laced with extra sand to promote fast drainage is best. Keep the soil on the dry side. Allow mix to dry out to a depth of two inches before irrigating again. **Light:** The plant can handle some direct summer sun. Give it maximum winter sun and bright, diffuse light the year round. It may adapt to less intense illumination with patience. **Temperature:** About 50° at night and 65° to 70° during the day is recommended. **Humidity:** Average. Freshen foliage daily with a mister or syringe in summer, weekly in winter. **Fertilizer:** Feed monthly from spring to fall with a complete fertilizer diluted to half strength. **Propagation:** From cuttings, by air layering, or from seeds.

Ligustrum lucidum 'Texanum'

Livistona *(Palms)*

Nativity: China and Australia

There are four varieties of the *Livistona* species which make durable, attractive houseplants when young. Most eventually must go outdoors (with the exception of *L. chinensis*) because of interior space limitations.

L. australis, commonly called, "Australian fan palm," at maturity in an outdoor location achieves sixty or more feet of height and has leaves five to six feet wide. Does very well indoors for many years.

L. chinensis, also called, "Chinese fan palm" and "fountain palm," grows even more slowly than *L. australis* and may never have to leave home. It is "self-cleaning," which means it throws off dead fronds as soon as they die. It has a very attractive crown of fan-shaped leaves which eventually reach seven feet in diameter. Probably the best of the four for indoor cultivation.

L. decipiens has, at maturity, leaves five or six feet in diameter which are deep green on top and have a faint blue cast underneath. Eventually reaches forty or more feet outdoors.

L. mariae is a dwarf, seldom growing taller than fourteen feet after many years. Leaves of older plants average three feet wide. Like *L. chinensis*, may not outgrow its indoor location—at least in your lifetime.

Use *Livistona* palms in any sunny or partially-sunny location. They make bold, interesting patterns against blank white walls and fit in nicely with a Spanish or contemporary decor.

Basic care. Acclimation: None required. **Soil:** A basic mix with extra sand and some horticultural charcoal is called for since the soil must be kept evenly moist during the growing season. **Light:** Some direct sun or filtered sun is good, but too much summer sun may be detrimental. Most grow well year-round in bright, diffuse light. **Temperature:** The normal household ranges work for all, but they seem to prefer cooler nights—around 55°. **Humidity:** Average, but all like a daily misting in hot weather, particularly if ventilation is poor. **Fertilizer:** Feed twice a year, spring and late summer, with a complete fertilizer at full strength. Freshly-potted palms should not be fertilized at all until the following year. **Propagation:** It is possible to propagate from seeds, but the wait is interminable. It's best to acquire new plants from the nursery.

Livistona chinensis

Mahonia

Common names: Leatherleaf (*M. beali*); Oregon holly-grape, or Holly-barberry (*M. aquifolium*).

Nativity: *M. aquifolium*: British Columbia, Northern California and Oregon; *M. beali*: Japan and Asia; *M. lomariifolia*: Asia

There are several varieties of this unusual, colorful shrub, but the three listed above are the ones easiest to adapt indoors and most often found in nurseries from the West Coast to New England. This is not a plant for those with toddlers or small children. All three have spiny-toothed leaves, much the same in appearance and pricking capacity as holly, which can deliver an annoying nip, as do certain cacti. Also it is not a plant for an entry or other heavy-traffic areas for the same reason. Its spiny tips can snag nylons and clothing. That's all the bad news. . . . The good news is that all three types of this shrub flower in early spring, sometimes in late winter, and then produce berries, if given adequate light.

M. aquifolium can grow to five or six feet and produces glossy, deep-green leaves four to ten inches long. In early spring, it blooms with clusters of lemon-yellow flowers two to three inches long, and these are followed by blue-black berries, which are edible. It responds well to pruning by branching rapidly.

M. beali attains heights, on the average, between seven and fifteen feet with thick, leathery leaflets three to five inches long. It produces pale yellow flowers with the heavy fragrance of lily of the valley in upright, spike-like clusters three to six inches long, usually in late winter or very early spring. Then there are black berries tinged with blue.

M. lomariifolia is the most familiar variety in temperate areas of the country. It isn't as hardy as *M. aquifolium*, which is hardy to occasional dips to 5° or 10° below zero, or *M. beali*, which is hardy as far north as upper New York state. It is, by far, the most attractive in appearance and structure of all the varieties, particularly for interior settings, and because of its tenderness and affinity for shade, adapts without difficulty indoors. It grows erect with small-branched stems and reaches ten feet with ideal conditions, but five feet is average indoors. It can be kept manageable indoors by pruning off growing tips. This works with all three varieties and encourages the development of branching. As the plant matures, it produces vertical branches near the base and clusters of twenty pairs of glossy leaflets symmetrically arranged along the branch. Yellow flowers appear in early spring in upright clusters at the tips of branch clusters. Bluish-black berries follow.

Use *Mahonias* in any bright, diffuse light situation, but keep them out of traffic patterns because of their spiny leaves. The plant likes kitchens and works well as an accent plant in living rooms.

Basic care. Acclimation: Even older specimens need no adaptation period. They move into any bright, cool, ventilated location immediately after repotting. **Soil:** All three varieties favor a fibrous acid soil that is kept evenly moist. Leaf mold and extra charcoal are two recommended soil amendments in the cultivation of *mahonias*. **Light:** *M. aquifolium* and *M. beali* need winter sun; *M. lomariifolia* prefers bright to medium-bright natural light, but can grow well in less illumination. Shield all three from direct summer sun. **Temperature:** The cool range produces best results—50° at night and 65° by day, but the plant can tolerate all interior levels, provided they are consistent. **Humidity:** Average. **Fertilizer:** Feed with a dilute acid fertilizer monthly from spring to late fall, beginning four to six months after purchase. **Propagation:** Propagate from seeds, suckers, air layering and cuttings.

Mahonia

Nicodemia diversifolia

Common name: Indoor oak
Nativity: Madagascar

Although it's not technically an oak—it gets its common name from the resemblance its leaves bears to those of the English oak—*N. diversifolia* is an interesting emmigrant from Madagascar where it grows much larger than the two feet you can expect indoors. Pinching out new growth promotes more bushiness, since its natural tendency is toward shrubbiness. There is a lot of appeal in the foliage which has a faint metallic blue cast. Since this plant is seldom available in its mature stage, a more striking display can be eventually achieved by potting up four or five specimens in a large container.

Use *N. diversifolia* in any bright, warm location, such as a kitchen.

Basic care. Acclimation: None required. **Soil:** An acid mix with extra sand and one tablespoon of ground limestone to a gallon of potting medium is recommended. Keep the soil evenly moist. **Light:** Some summer sun, maximum winter sun, or bright, diffuse light the year around. **Temperature:** Prefers an environment on the warm side—65° minimum at night and 80° during the day, with good ventilation. Will adapt well to the normal household ranges. **Humidity:** Average. Mist once a day in hot weather. Keep leaves free of dust. **Fertilizer:** Feed every month from spring to fall with a complete fertilizer at half strength.

Propagation: From stem cuttings which root easily, in spring.

Nicodemia diversifolia

Olea europaea

Common name: Olive tree
Nativity: Eastern Mediterranean

Yes, Virginia—with proper care, olive trees can be grown indoors and, if pollinated by hand, will bear fruit. This is the classical olive tree which has been cultivated for its fruit and oil since Biblical times. Outdoors, it grows to thirty-five feet and, indoors, the limit is the

height of your ceiling. It can be controlled by selective pruning and, as a juvenile tree, shaped to grow with a single trunk or several. If given ample sun, it will produce a riot of fragrant white flowers which should be pollinated with a small brush if you wish to have olives. Even without blossoms or fruit, *O. europaea* makes a durable and attractive tree with its willowy, gray-green foliage two to three inches long.

Olea europaea (Olive tree)

Use *O. europaea* in any sunny location.

Basic care. Acclimation: Specimens three years old or older may require a brief acclimation as described for sun-loving plants in the chapter on adaptation. Seedlings and younger trees should adjust without difficulty in a sunny, well-ventilated location. **Soil:** A basic mix with extra sand and one tablespoon of ground limestone per gallon of potting medium is recommended. *O. europaea* needs deeper soil than most, so you should jump the plant two pot sizes. Let it dry to a depth of two inches before irrigating again. **Light:** Requires summer and winter sun to thrive, but will survive in bright, diffuse light. **Temperature:** A night temperature of 50° and a day temperature of 70° or under are ideal. **Humidity:** Average. Mist in hot weather and provide good ventilation. **Fertilizer:** Feed in March and again in June with a complete fertilizer at full strength. **Propagation:** From stem cuttings any time of the year.

NOTE: An easier "olive tree"—this one grown primarily for its long-lived, jasmine-scented flowers—is the Asian *Osmanthus fragrans*, or sweet olive. As a juvenile plant, it tends to be spindly, but established plants (in five-gallon cans) are sturdier and have denser, glossy oval foliage. At maturity, six feet can be expected indoors. *O. fragrans* does best if kept slightly pot-bound. This encourages greater floral production and longer retention of blooms. To promote bushiness, pinch out new growth periodically. Pot up in a basic soil mix and keep it evenly moist. A sunny location is best, particularly for inducing blooms, but bright, diffuse light will suffice. Keep *O. fragrans* cool—50°-55° at night and not much above 68° during the day. Misting helps during the hot summer days. Feed twice a year, in spring and summer, with a complete fertilizer diluted to half strength. Propagate from cuttings.

Osmanthus heterophyllus

Common name: Holly-leaf osmanthus
Nativity: Primarily Asia

There are several varieties of the *O. heterophyllus* species, all of which are adaptable indoors, but the variety 'Variegatus' (illustrated) seems happiest indoors.

O.h. '*Gulftide*' has deep green, prominently-toothed leaves compactly set on its branches. May grow to five feet indoors.

O. h. '*Illicifolius,*' or "false holly," closely resembles 'Gulftide' but grows more erect and may reach six or seven feet indoors. In good light, aromatic white flowers may appear in spring.

O. h. '*Rotundifolius*' is more compact and smaller and may only achieve three feet of height indoors. Leaves are smaller, rounder.

O.h. '*Variegatus*' is a durable, easily acclimated variety characterized by spiny leaves two to three inches long which are dull green in the center and edged with white. It should grow (slowly) to five feet indoors.

Use *O. heterophyllus* in any location that gets good light, even some sun. Tolerant of both cold and drafts.

Basic care. Acclimation: None required. Most are shade-fanciers and move to a bright, diffuse natural light location without difficulty. **Soil:** A basic mix with extra sand kept just barely moist works well for all. However, acid or slightly acid soil seems to produce equally good results. **Light:** Bright, diffuse is recommended, but all can take (and may do better with) some direct summer sun, except unfiltered sun through a west window in mid-summer. All three benefit from full winter sun. **Temperature:** Night, 55° or cooler; day, 68° or slightly warmer, with good ventilation. **Humidity:** Average. Misting the leaves a few times a week enhances their appearance. **Fertilizer:** Most seem to do well if fed only in spring and again in summer with a complete fertilizer, organic or chemical, at full strength. **Propagation:** Propagate from stem cuttings or by air layering. If you prune the plants, do so in early spring.

Osmanthus heterophyllus '*Variegatus*'

Phoenix *(date palms)*

Nativity: Canary Islands; Burma

Phoenix canariensis. Native to the Canary Islands, it grows to sixty feet outdoors with a frond spread of forty feet or more growing in typical palm fashion from a stout trunk. *P. canariensis* eventually must go outside because of its space requirements, but it can be kept indoors for many years.

Phoenix roebeleinii, native to Asia and particularly Laos, may be a better choice for those who become emotionally involved with their plants and would find it difficult to part with one, as is inevitably necessary with *P. canariensis*. *P. roebeleinii*, or more commonly pigmy date palm, is an extremely slow grower which may reach six feet indoors but averages only two feet. It produces delicate, arching fronds about two feet long adorned with leaves which average eight inches in length.

Use both in bright or sunny windows (diffuse sunlight by using a thin curtain between window and plant). Both suffer in dimly illuminated interior locations.

Basic care. Acclimation: Both adapt well indoors with little if any softening off. Several we've tried in bright windows direct from the nursery adapted without difficulty. The secret is to keep them well watered and misted during the first two weeks. **Soil:** Both require a basic soil mix that drains well; well-rotted manure added to the recipe is highly desirable, but not imperative. Keep the soil very damp with both varieties, except in winter, but make sure they're not water-logged or sitting in a bog. *P. roebeleinii*, particularly during growing season, likes hard-packed, almost wet soil. **Light:** The plants need full winter sun and very bright natural light the rest of the year; they will suffer with anything less. **Temperature:** Both like their environment on the warm side—65° to 70° at night, 75° to 85° by day—but will settle for cooler or warmer levels. **Humidity:** Average. Mist daily, if possible, especially during the hottest days of summer. **Fertilizer:** Feed both monthly from spring through summer with a complete fertilizer, starting four to six months after acquiring the plants. **Propagation:** From seeds, or with *P. roebeleinii*, from suckers produced at the base of the plant.

Phoenix canariensis

Pittosporum tobira

Common names: Australian laurel; mock orange
Nativity: South Sea Islands, Australia

Another eminently adaptable plant seldom tried indoors, *P. tobira* does better indoors than many tropical houseplants, particularly if it summers outdoors on a shaded patio or balcony. Its two-inch to four-inch-long foliage has a waxy sheen with rounded tips and grows in a pattern reminiscent of rosettes. It is a shrubby plant and is generally used in hedges, like the waxleaf privet. Under ideal conditions, it grows to ten feet (fifteen feet outdoors), but because it has an ungainly appearance if unpruned, it usually requires heading back in early spring before new growth begins. Although it may not

do so indoors, it blooms with white or yellow flowers whose fragrance is similar in bouquet to orange blossoms. These eventually give way to round, green seed pods that brown off in late fall or early winter, and because the species is self-sowing, crack open to release their seeds (up to twelve seeds per pod), which are brilliant orangish-red. The plant requires re-potting only every three or four years. Top dress annually to revitalize the soil.

Use *P. tobira* in any bright, diffuse-light situation. It is hardy enough for cool sunporches and tolerant enough for warm kitchens.

Basic care. Acclimation: The plant should adapt well without difficulty if kept slightly cool, out of the sun, but in bright, diffuse light, and on the dry side for the first two weeks after bringing it inside. Raise the humidity to ease the shock of moving from a natural to an artificial environment. **Soil:** Basic mix slightly on the acid side is best. An extra cup or two of leaf mold added to the basic formula should do it. **Light:** Bright, diffuse the year around, but the plant can tolerate some summer sun filtered through a thin curtain and likes full winter sun. It may be moved to a dimmer light location the second year. **Temperature:** Ideal levels are 55° at night and 65° by day, but *P. tobira* quickly adapts to cooler or warmer levels. **Humidity:** Average. Mist daily in hot weather and once or twice a week during the winter. **Fertilizer:** The plant can get by with only two feedings each year with an acid fertilizer at full strength—once in spring and again in summer. **Propagation:** From cuttings, seeds, or by air layering.

Pittosporum tobira

Platycerium

Common name: Staghorn fern
Nativity: South Sea Islands, Australia

Platycerium probably haven't changed much since the first living organism slithered out of the primordial slime onto land millions of years ago. The staghorn, like other *Platycerium*, is an epiphytic member of the fern family, which means it obtains nourishment by absorbing organic matter from the air. In its native habitat it grows on the bark of trees, producing two kinds of fronds: the staghorn-shaped fronds, from whence it gets its common name, hang down two to three feet and are fertile; and the overlapping, sterile basal fronds, which anchor the plant to its support and gather organic nutrients to sustain life. The plantlets (pups) which appear among the basal fronds can be removed for propagation or left on the plant to produce a really impressive specimen. Staghorns have some drawbacks: they're slow growers, by comparison with most plants; they're better suited to greenhouse cultivation because of their high humidity requirement; and they're expensive in the larger sizes. The plant illustrated is about ten years old. Its fronds measure three feet long and it sold for $85. However smaller plants can be obtained for under ten dollars.

Use staghorns wherever you can provide consistent high humidity and light, such as a bathroom which gets very bright light.

Basic care. Acclimation: None is required. Most staghorns are grown under lath or in the greenhouse in colder climes. Simply keep the "anchor" moist, mist frequently, and provide bright, diffuse illumination with no direct sun. **Soil:** *Platycerium* are grown on bark-covered wood, cork bark, or a combination of sphagnum and peat mosses, among other materials. This should be kept moist by bucket-soaking the plant base once a week. Never let it dry out. **Light:** The plant requires brilliant illumination. A north window exposure works well. Direct sun rays can burn the delicate foliage, but a thin curtain between the plant and the window will filter out the harmful rays. The plant fails or deteriorates in dim light.

Temperature: It does best in a range of 55° to 60° at night and 65° to 75° by day.

Humidity: High humidity means the difference between success and failure. If a staghorn dies indoors, nine times out of ten it was the victim of hot, dry air. Soak its organic

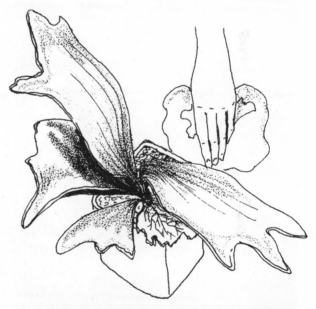

support once a week and mist daily. In winter, keep its fronds washed to remove dust and other airborne contaminants. **Fertilizer:** None. This plant can fend for itself. **Propagation:** Take pups (young plantlets) at any time of year and affix them with wire to a moss or bark support that has been thoroughly soaked in water.

Platycerium "pups"

Podocarpus

Nativity: Asia, Africa, Australia, and South America

Four varieties of *Podocarpus* adapt well indoors and grow into major foliage plants. All can be purchased as field-grown specimens already of substantial size.

P. gracilior (Sometimes labeled *P. elongatus*). Commonly called fern pine. The foliage characteristics change considerably as the fern pine achieves maturity, but in the seedling stage, it is dark green to blue-green and about an inch and a half long. It slowly grows indoors to six or seven feet (seventy-five feet is common in its native Africa).

P. macrophyllus, or yew pine, produces vibrant green leaves about four inches long and also grows to about six feet indoors (forty feet outdoors).

P. macrophyllus maki, or Chinese podocarpus, is one of the best of the species for indoor cultivation. It can take direct sun and cold drafts in stride. Its foliage is densely set, soft deep green, one and a half to three inches long and a quarter-inch to half an inch wide.

P. m. nagi, or Japanese podocarpus, is a spreader, but it also attains impressive heights after a few years. It, like the *maki*, does well indoors.

Use all varieties to create bold patterns against a blank white wall, or like bamboo, to provide a natural privacy screen for undraped windows. The plants can go outdoors on a shaded balcony or patio in mild weather, then back inside in the late fall, before the first frost. Prune and shape in earliest spring, before vigorous growth period begins.

Basic care. Acclimation: None is required if you can provide a bright or partially sunny spot. **Soil:** The plant does well in a basic soil mix with one to two tablespoons of limestone added to each gallon of planting medium. Keep the soil barely moist and don't worry about potting on. All varieties can go for a number of years in the same container. Annual top dressing helps prolong fertility of the soil. **Light:** All but *P. gracilior* appreciate some direct sun in summer and maximum winter sun. *P. gracilior* suffers in full sun and likes bright, diffuse light. All will thrive with a north or south window exposure or under a skylight. If the needles begin to pale (not yellow), the light level is insufficient; if they begin to yellow, the tree is going into the incipient stages of chlorosis. An iron additive diluted to the recommended strength should correct this overnight. **Temperature:** None of the four is too particular about the temperature level. Ideal levels are 45° to 55° at night and 70° to 80° by day, but all can survive lower and higher temperatures. **Humidity:** Average. Misting once a week is beneficial. **Fertilizer:** Feed twice a year in April and August with a complete fertilizer at full strength. **Propagation:** From stem cuttings or seeds.

Podocarpus

Pseudopanax lessonii

Common name: False panax
Nativity: New Zealand

This New Zealand import is fast becoming the substitute plant for Schefflera (*Brassaia actinophylla*). Except for its blunt-tipped, partially-serrated leaves, it closely resembles the Schefflera, or "umbrella tree," in structure, growth habits and culture requirements. Scheffleras are extremely susceptible to spider mite infestation—so much so, in fact, that many growers are no longer cultivating them—while *P. lessonii* is pest resistant and tolerant of abuse. In its natural habitat, *P. lessonii* grows into an attractive tree twenty feet tall. In temperate areas of the United States, fifteen feet is average after a number of years. Indoors, it can grow to twelve feet (we have one in our living room at least this tall), under optimum growing conditions. An oddity of the plant is that new foliage may be encased in a clear, glossy residue which looks very much like the honeydew secretion of aphids. This is a natural phenomenon peculiar to the species. It can, unfortunately, cause some foliage to become deformed, since the residue hardens to a set-glue consistency. Usually, it can be picked off by hand, but sometimes the leaf comes off with it.

Use *P. lessonii* virtually anywhere short of a sunny window location. Does well any place that gets medium to bright, diffuse light.

Basic care. Acclimation: Absolutely none required. Move immediately indoors without any special acclimatizing period. **Soil:** A basic, fast-draining mix kept on the dry side. Let the soil dry out to a depth of two inches before watering again. **Light:** Does best in bright, diffuse light—near a north window, for example—but tolerant of lower levels. Can't take summer sun, but may adapt to full winter sun. **Temperature:** Adjusts well to all interior levels. With higher temperatures, provide good ventilation. Protect from excessive chilling in winter. **Humidity:** High humidity in summer. Mist frequently. **Fertilizer:** Feed monthly spring to fall with a complete fertilizer diluted at half strength. **Propagation:** By air layering mature specimens.

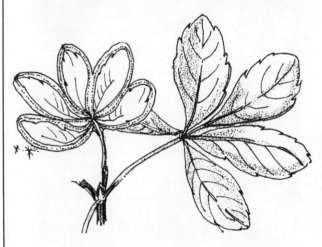

Pseudopanax lessonii

Sedum

Nativity: Primarily Mexico

Sedum is a member of the succulent family which, loosely speaking, means the many species of cacti without spines. Smaller varieties have long been collected by cacti fanciers for indoor desert gardens, and—probably the best known of all—*Sedum morganianum*, or "burro's tail," is an old standby in many Californian, Southwestern and Mexican homes. Like cacti, most sedum varieties and other succulents, as well, bloom with many unusual floral patterns in spring and summer, if given ample sun.

S. dendroideum and its big brother, *S. praealtum*, are multibranching spreaders with round, thick leaves which average an inch-and-a-half in length and have bronzy overtones. *S. dendroideum* grows to about two and a half feet, producing vibrant yellow flowers while *S. praealtum* attains heights of three, four and sometimes five feet, with pale yellow blooms.

S. morganianum's habit of producing ropes of foliage which, after several years, can reach four feet, makes it a natural for a sturdily-supported hanging basket. It's compactly set, overlapping, gray-green leaves have a faint blue cast. Flowers are pink but these usually don't appear unless ample sun is provided. The foliage is very delicate and too much handling will break off the foliage tassels. (These can be rooted again in moist sand or by simply sticking the ends back into the pot soil.) For this reason, it's a good idea not to repot this specimen.

S. sieboldii comes to us from Asia. It's single stemmed and carries several three inch, bluish-gray, fleshy leaves topped in late summer by pink blossoms.

Use sedum in a window location that gets direct sun for a few hours each day.

Basic care. Acclimation: None required. **Soil:** Use the succulent mix described in Chapter 5. Keep the mix on the dry side year round. If these and other succulents are not getting enough water, their leaves begin to wrinkle. This is your cue to increase either the frequency or volume of irrigation. Too much water will rot these plants. **Light:** All do best in direct summer sun (with good ventilation) for a few hours daily and all the winter sun they can get. Most will accept bright, diffuse light and a few will struggle along with only medium light. **Temperature:** All like the cool range of 50° to 55° at night and 65° to 70° by day, but adjust to virtually any interior range. **Humidity:** Low. Twice a year, wipe the foliage (of all except *S. morganianum*) with a damp cloth or paper towel to remove dust. **Fertilizer:** Feed twice a year with a complete fertilizer at full strength, in February and July. **Propagation:** Leaf and stem cuttings root easily in moist sand anytime of year.

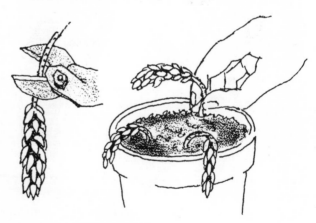

Sedum

Ternstroemia gymnanthera

Common name: Ternstroemia japonica
Nativity: Tropics

An attractive, easily adaptable shrub which is rarely tried indoors but which does quite well inside. Although it attains a height of about eighteen feet outdoors after several years, three to four feet indoors is average. Its glossy, oval leaves closely resemble *F. r. nitida* in the juvenile stage and are about two to three inches long. New foliage is usually bronze-maroon and eventually turns deep green.

Pinching out new growth promotes a shrubby appearance, but—if you prefer a more tree-like specimen, leave new growth. Although it probably won't bloom indoors, *T. gymnanthera* produces aromatic yellow flowers in early summer and these are followed by crimson, berry-like fruit which, like the fruit of the *Pittosporum*, split open to expose glossy black seeds which may be used in propagation.

Use *T. gymnanthera* as a focal-point plant in or near a brightly illuminated window. Bushy foliage makes it ideal as a privacy screen for an undraped window.

Basic care. Acclimation: Juvenile shrubs grown under lath require no acclimation period. Move directly to a bright window location and keep humidity high for the first month. **Soil:** An acid mix kept barely moist. Allow soil to dry out to a depth of two inches between irrigations. **Light:** Does best in bright, diffuse light year round, but likes full winter sun. **Temperature:** A range of 55° to 60° at night and under 70° during the day is recommended. Will eventually adapt to normal interior ranges, but prefers a slightly cool environment. **Humidity:** Low humidity in winter and medium humidity in summer. A daily misting of foliage is beneficial to counteract the effects of hot, dry interior air and to preserve the attractive appearance of the glossy leaves. **Fertilizer:** Feed monthly from spring to fall with an acid fertilizer at full strength. **Propagation:** From seeds or with new plants (inexpensive) from the nursery.

Ternstroemia gymnanthera

Trachycarpus fortunei

Common name: European windmill palm; windmill palm
Nativity: China and Japan

The windmill palm is an ideal container palm which grows into an impressive plant very rapidly if it is given good light, adequate water, and fertilizer. Outdoors it attains heights of twenty-five and thirty feet; indoors, ten feet is usually tops, and six feet is average, after several years of growth. It grows in typical palm fashion, with palmate leaves, which at maturity measure three to four feet across, carried on spiny fronds about two feet long. The stout trunk is adorned with characteristic hairy fiber. Two other family members which may be tried are *T. martianus*, which—although it grows taller—is slower-growing; and *T. takil*, which is even slower, with a heavier trunk. *T. takil* should sit happily in its original pot for many years. Both will thrive with the identical care given *T. fortunei*.

Use *Trachycarpus* to carry a blank wall which gets good light or a large, naturally well-lit entry. Fronds which get in the way of pedestrian traffic can be tied back.

Basic care. Acclimation: Field-grown plants adapt well and can usually go from the nursery to an indoor window. Keep the plant well watered. The lowest fronds may die off immediately. These should be trimmed off to encourage faster top growth. If top fronds begin to die off, move the plant outside in shade and withhold water for two weeks —windmill palms are hardy to 15°. The plant should recover. Try it again indoors in a cooler spot, but still provide bright, diffuse light. **Soil:** The plant needs a deep, fibrous soil laced with sand to promote good drainage. Keep the soil evenly moist through the hot months, then cut back water in winter, but never let the soil completely dry out. **Light:** Give full winter sun and bright natural light the rest of the year. The plant suffers in dim light. **Temperature:** The cool range: 50° to 55° at night; 65° to 75° by day; but the plant adapts to other ranges, especially on the cool side. **Humidity:** Average humidity. Wash fronds and leaves monthly to freshen. **Fertilizer:** Begin feeding monthly four to six months after acquisition with a complete fertilizer, spring to fall. **Propagation:** Propagate from seeds, which take up to seven months for germination. It is usually better to buy another palm, which will cost $1.49 to $2.98 for a specimen in a one-gallon can.

Trachycarpus fortunei

Viburnum

Nativity: Asia, Europe and N. America

Viburnum encompasses an extensive group of deciduous and evergreen shrubs. The evergreen species are *V. cinnamomifolium, V. davidii, V. japonicum* (illustrated), *V. odoratissimum, V. propinquum, V. suspensum,* and *V. tinus*. Of these, the four best indoor candidates are:

V. cinnamomifolium. May grow to six or seven feet indoors with a significant spread. Its foliage, at maturity, is impressive—vibrant green leaves five or six inches long and three inches wide. May bloom with white, delicately-scented flowers emerging from pinkish buds in early spring.

V. japonicum. Probably the best for indoor cultivation, you can expect leathery deep-green leaves about four to five inches long, six feet of height and—with some pruning back of new growth—thick, bushy growth and considerable spread. May bloom in spring with clusters of aromatic flowers.

V. suspensum, or "Sandankwa viburnum," should not exceed five feet indoors. Leaves are ovate and three to four inches long and quite attractive. Good, thick foliage production. Flowers, which may appear in spring, are white and heavily-scented.

V. tinus, or "Laurestinus," will grow more tree-like as it matures to about five feet (indoors). Leaves are smaller and tend to curl down at the edges. Like *V. cinnamomifolium,* white flowers emerge from pink buds anytime from late fall or early winter to spring.

Use *Viburnum* in any partially-sunny situation where the night temperature is cool (below 55°).

Basic care. Acclimation: Juvenile plants should require no acclimation. Older, established plants may need an acclimation period, but try the specimen indoors first. If it continues to thrive after three or four weeks, just keep doing what you're doing. **Soil:** All four seem to prefer a slightly acid soil kept evenly moist until fall, then barely moist. **Light:** Sun, summer and winter, produces the best results, but all should survive with bright, diffuse light year-round. In summer, provide adequate ventilation for plants sitting in direct sun. A direct western summer sun exposure may be too intense. **Temperature:** The ideal ranges are 55° night and not much above 68° day. Seedling specimens can be easily adapted to most household ranges. **Humidity:** Average. Mist once a day in hot weather. Wash off leaves once a week through the winter. **Fertilizer:** Feed twice a year, in spring and again in summer, with an acid fertilizer at full strength. **Propagation:** From seeds, cuttings or by air layering.

Viburnum japonicum

Sources for Seeds, Plants and Supplies

Seeds

W. Atlee Burpee Seed Co.
370 Burpee Building
Philadelphia, Pennsylvania 19132
 also
Clinton, Iowa 52733
Riverside, California 92502

Burgess Seed & Plant Co.
Box 1140
67 E. Battle Creek Street
Galesburg, Michigan 49053

Gurney Seed & Nursery Co.
1448 Page Street
Yankton, South Dakota 57078

George Park Seed Co., Inc.
P.O. Box 31
Greenwood, South Carolina 29646

Girard Nursery
Geneva, Ohio 44041

Cacti and other Succulents

Cactiflor
Box 787
Belen, New Mexico 87002

Hummel's Exotic Gardens
3926 Park Drive
Carlsbad, California 92008

Johnson Cactus Gardens
Box 207
Bonsall, California 92003
 also
Box 458
Paramount, California 90723

Plants, Shrubs, and Supplies

Alberts & Merkle Bros., Inc.
P.O. Box 537
2210 S. Federal Highway
Boynton Beach, Florida 33435

Fruitland Nurseries
Augusta, Georgia 30901

Rod McLellan Co.
1450 El Camino Real
So. San Francisco, California 94080

Roehrs Exotic Nurseries
Route 2, Box 144
Farmingdale, New Jersey 07727

Julius Roehrs Co.
East Rutherford, New Jersey 07073

Tropical Paradise Greenhouses
8825 W. 79th Street
Overland Park, Kansas 66200

Glossary of Horticultural Terms

Alga (AL′ jeh), pl. **Algae** (AL′ gee) Aquatic, simple celled plants containing chlorophyll that are part of the first group of plants termed *Thallophyta*. The green scum on terra cotta pots is the fungi form and grows on leeched-out chemical salts on the clay pots.

Amendment A soil conditioner, such as peat moss, manure, perlite, vermiculite, pumice, and sand, that is used to improve the moisture holding capacity or drainage efficiency in potting soil.

Bract A small, modified leaf with or without a stem.

Bromeliad (broh-MEE′ lih-ade) A genus of perennials, members of the pineapple family, found primarily in Central America and South America.

Callus (CAL′ us) The dried covering which forms over plant tissues from which parts have been severed.

Chelating agent (KEE′ late-ing) A chemical which makes an element, such as iron, immediately available to a plant's system.

Chlorophyll (KLOR′ o-fill) The green coloring matter in plants.

Chlorosis (kluh-ROE′ sus) Loss of chlorophyll in plants characterized by paling of normal green coloring to yellow.

Complete fertilizer To be termed a complete fertilizer, a plant food must contain a balance of the three primary nutrients of nitrogen, phosphorous and potassium, or potash.

Cultivar (CULT′ ih-vahr) A botanical variety of a species which originated and has persisted under cultivation.

Cuttings Leaf or stem sections of a plant which are taken for propagation. They are rooted in water, sand, peat moss, soil, or other rooting media, then potted up.

Deciduous (dee-SID′ you-us) The opposite of evergreen. Any tree or shrub termed deciduous loses its foliage seasonally.

Degradable (de-GRADE′ uh-bull) Any chemical or material which can be reduced in amount or strength. A degradable insecticide, for example, is one that eventually loses its "kill potential" or is weakened by time, dilution, decomposition, or dispersion in the soil.

Dormancy (DOR′ man-see) A vital period of rest and inactivity in plants which allows them to rejuvenate. Excessive cold can induce and prolong dormancy.

Dry well A layer of clay shards, gravel, pebbles, rocks, or other material, placed in the bottom of a container which does not have a drainage hole, into which excess water may drain, thereby preventing soured soil and root rot.

Evergreen Any plant, shrub, or tree which retains its foliage the year around.

Feeder roots Minute, thread-like roots which branch out from primary roots to collect the nutrients and moisture which sustain a plant.

Friable (FRY′ uh-bull) A soil characteristic in which the soil, although moist, retains a loose character and resists packing. All potting soil should be friable.

Genus (GEE′ nus), pl. **Genera** (JEN′ er-uh) A plant group, or family, consisting of closely related species having similar structural characteristics. The first word in a plant's botanical name is the *genus*, the second word indicates the kind or *species* name. For example, *Ficus* is the genus to which all figs belong and *benjamina* tells you what kind of *Ficus*.

Hardpan A detrimental soil condition in which the individual soil particles are so packed together that the soil is virtually impenetrable. The condition is common in pots containing extremely fine soil which contains no fibrous material, such as peat moss, bits of bark or wood, charcoal, or other amendments. Overhead watering over a period of months compacts the soil into a "cement" which admits no water, air, or roots.

Jumping (a plant)   The term is used to describe moving a plant up to a pot too large for its root structure. This causes a plant to expend energy filling the new soil with roots, to the detriment of new growth of the top foliage.

Leeching (or leaching)   In terra cotta pots, the action of moisture and minerals passing through the porous sides of the pot.

Loam (LOME′)   Loosely, any soil that is a mixture of both clay and sand as well as some organic matter.

Microclimate (MIKE′ roe-cly-mut)   Literally, a smaller climate inside a larger climate. More specifically, a climate in a small area which is different from the surrounding climate because of certain conditions. For example, a plant whose pot is sitting on water-covered pebbles is living in a microclimate in which a higher humidity level is produced by moisture evaporating from the pebbles. Terrariums and bottle gardens are also good examples of microclimates.

Mulch (MULCH′)   Any material, such as leaves, manure, leaf mold, or straw, that is spread over the top soil around a plant or shrub to hold in moisture and prevent roots from drying out. Outdoors, mulching also prevents frost damage.

Node (NODE′)   The joint on a stem or branch where leaves and buds originate.

Offset   An infant plantlet which grows from the base of the mother plant and can usually be separated for propagation.

Organic fertilizer   Any fertilizer basically composed of once-living matter. The sources include the various animal manures, blood and bones, fish and fish oils, tobacco, and peat.

Osmosis (oss-MOE′ sis)   The complex process of absorption of one liquid into another through a thin membrane. Water collected by a plant's roots is passed through the semi-permeable membranes of plant cells one by one. This process is called osmosis.

Ovate (OH′ vate)   Of foliage, having an oval shape.

Palmate (POL′ mate)   Of foliage, divided like the fingers and palm of a hand.

Panicle (PAN′ ih-cul)   A loose, diversely branching cluster, usually of flowers.

Peat moss   Composed primarily of decayed sphagnum moss.

Photosynthesis (foto-SIN′ theh-sis)   The process, still not fully understood, by which a plant's foliage uses sunlight as energy (with chlorophyll as the catalyst) to manufacture sugars and starches from carbon dioxide absorbed from the air, along with water and inorganic salts. The word itself is derived from two Greek words: *Photo*, meaning "light" and *Synthesis*, meaning "to put together."

Pot-bound   A condition in which the roots of a plant have become densely packed or outgrown their container and are unable to function normally.

Potting on   Moving a plant to a larger container to provide adequate room for continuing root development.

Respiration   The process by which plants assimilate oxygen and expend water vapor and waste products, such as carbon dioxide.

Salts   In potted plants, sodium nitrate, which is used as a source of nitrogen in fertilizer, often leeches through clay pots to form a white crust on the outside.

Sphagnum moss (SFAG′ num)   A moss-like plant which grows in bogs and is highly water-absorbent. It is used as a mulch, as a propagating medium, and as a soil amendment.

Stoma (STOH′ muh, pl. **Stomata** (STOH′ muh-tuh)   Minute orifices, or pores, in the epidermis of leaves which enable a plant to carry on respiration and/or transpiration.

Sucker   A shoot that develops from the soil at the base of a plant, instead of from the stem.

Systemic (siss-TEM′ ic)   Affecting the entire system. For example, a systemic insecticide is taken up by the roots of a plant and carried throughout its system, from the feeder roots to the tips of the foliage.

Transpiration   A naturally regulated process in which excess water, in vaporized form, is expended by the leaves of a plant through the stomata.

Bibliography

Katharine M. P. Cloud, "Evergreens for Every State," Chilton Company, Philadelphia.

Chuck Crandall, "Success With Houseplants," Chronicle Books, San Francisco.

James Underwood Crockett, "Foliage House Plants," Time-Life Books, New York.

Thalassa Cruso, "Making Things Grow," Alfred A. Knopf, New York.

A. B. Graf, "Exotica," Roehrs Company, East Rutherford, New Jersey.

Elda Haring, "The Complete Book of Growing Plants from Seed," Hawthorn Books, Inc., New York.

Jack Kramer, "1,000 Beautiful Houseplants and How to Grow Them," Wm. Morrow and Co., New York.

Elvin McDonald, "The World Book of House Plants," World Publishing Company.

"Sunset Western Garden Book," edited by *Sunset* Magazine and Book Co., Menlo Park, California.

Index

R

Re-potting, 25-32
Respiration, 37, definition, 171
Rhizome, 71
Root divisions, 47, 50
"Rootone," 29
Root rot, 26, 29, 62, 63
Rotenone, 60
Rubber tree, 35, 47, 51, 123
Runners, 47, 49

S

Salts (mineral), definition, 171
Sand, 43
Sandankwa viburnum, 167
Sawdust, 43
Scale (insect), 57, 58, 60
Screwpine, 49
Seeds (techniques in propagation), 47-49
Sedum, description, illustration and care, 161
Sedum dendroideum, S.morganianum, S. praealtum, S.sieboldii, 161
Sheffleras, 44, 51, 117, 159
Silk oak, 47
Soil (description of types), 43-44
Spathephyllum, 26, 35
Sphagnum moss, 27, 37, 48, 50, 51, 75, definition, 171
Stern's "Miracle-Gro," "Miracid," 39
Stoma, stomata, 38, definition, 171
Stump sprout, 54
Succulents, 44
Suckers, 49, definition, 171
Sulphur, 38, (mildew control), 63
"Supersoil," 43
Sweet bay, 137
Systematic poison, 58, definition, 171

T

Tangelo, 99
Tasmanian tree fern, 75
Taylor, Gordon Rattray, 57
TDE, 57
Ternstroemia gymnanthera, description, illustration and care, 163
Texas privet, 139
Threadleaf, 111
Thrips, 13, 60
Top dressing (soil), 30, 44
Toxaphene, 57
Trachycarpus fortunei, description, illustration and care, 165
Trachycarpus martianus, T.takil, 165
Transpiration, definition, 171
Transplant shock, 51
TSP, 31

U

Umbrella tree, 51, 159

V

Vaporizers, 38
Vermiculite, 43, 48, 50
Viburnum, description, illustration and care, 167
Viburnum cinnamomifolium, V.davidii, V.japonicum, V.odoratissimum, V.propinquum, V.suspensum, V.tinus, 167
Vitamin B-1, 28, 51

W

Water (types), 36-37
Weeping Chinese banyan, 121
Weeping fig, 121
Whiteflies, 57, 60
Windmill palm, 165

Y

Yew, 50
Yew pine, 157

Z

Zinc, 38